The Lily
and the
Flame

Lynette Rees

Acknowledgements

Thanks to Heather Copping for providing the name *The Rosie Lea* for the tea room in this story. A very apt name indeed. Congratulations on winning the newsletter competition!

Dedication

To Helen Snow for your invaluable help and support with this book and the two previous books in the Rags to Riches series. Many thanks too for being such a good friend!

Chapter One

Early Spring 1885
England
"Unfortunate Timing"

Chatterton Court stood loud and proud on the top of the hill overlooking the English village of Foxbridge. The new owner had made it his own over time and was very proud of its sweep of green lawns, its immaculate colourful flower beds and semi-circle of wooded land surrounding the property. It was a sight to behold indeed for the odd visitor, but today the owner had something else on his mind other than his estate and his great wealth which he had just inherited officially that very same day. The official documentation had been signed, sealed and delivered, yet a matter of the heart was at stake here and as far as Archie Pomfrey was concerned, his heart would always win over his head, every time.

He gazed out of the large French window where he could see down below onto the village which was a rich wool weaving and market town. Rodden Row in Foxbridge was a long line of millworkers stone cottages with thatched roofs, whose inhabitants had worked for his father. The father he had never even known nor met. In fact, most people in Foxbridge had either been employed at the wool mill or else worked as farmers or in the little shops on Pomfrey land. And offset from Rodden Row there was a scattering of little cottages and farmhouses here and there in a higgledy-piggedly fashion. Near the old Norman church was a fast-flowing river which set the village apart from Crownley by dividing the area in two. Those living in Foxbridge tended to consider themselves as a cut above those in Crownley but nevertheless, there was no umbrage as such between both villages which were quaint in their own sort of way.

His mind turned to the upcoming visit from a special guest and he smiled as he thought of her. Had eleven years really passed since he'd first encountered Lucy when he was little more than a street urchin and she a scullery maid at the coaching inn? How things had changed so much for the pair of them when it was discovered he was the son of Sir Richard Pomfrey and as his eldest son had died in a riding accident, he was the last surviving heir of the dynasty. Lucy, when she discovered her real heritage and who her mother and grandmother were, had been shocked yet pleasantly surprised. They both had a rags to riches story to tell and it wasn't over yet, not by a long chalk.

He well remembered his excitement when he'd arranged a little party back then at Huntington Hall, his uncle's estate, for all his friends. Lucy had stepped down from the carriage, looking enchanting as her chocolate brown eyes shone as she'd smiled at him. He even remembered what she'd worn that afternoon: a lemon silk dress that made her look so grown up, matching with the same colour bonnet over her lustrous chestnut brown curls. And around her shoulders, she'd worn a white lace wrap.

To see her stood before him had stolen his breath away, she'd looked a proper little lady. Uncle Walter had been prepared to offer her a position at the house as a kitchen maid. He so hoped she'd accept at the time, he hadn't liked the thought of her staying at that coaching house, but then he'd discovered she had good fortune of her own when she'd been informed that Adella (the name inscribed on her silver locket left with her when she was abandoned as a baby) was her mother and Lady Fanshaw her grandmother.

She'd smiled shyly at Archie and he'd taken her white-gloved hand in his own to help her down from the carriage. He'd so wanted to kiss her on that pretty little porcelain-like cheek of hers, but there were too many eyes on them that afternoon.

They'd kept up their friendship and things had never been more than a kiss on the cheek or the holding of hands, but today his heart beat a little faster as he had a proposition for her. He was going to ask her to marry him.

***

Lucy was dressed and about to depart as her carriage waited outside on the drive way when her mother called after her. 'Lucy, darling!'

She turned and gazed at her mother who after all these years was still a beautiful woman, her dark hair piled up on her head in an elegant fashion, with soft tendrils at her face. That's what love did for you, she thought. Marrying Nathaniel Knight was the best thing her mother had ever done. Their marriage was one of true devotion and plain for all to see.

'Mama?'

Her mother's eyes weren't glittering as was usual, there was some concern behind them and that troubled her.

Slightly out of breath because she'd been chasing after her daughter, Mama said the words that Lucy wished she could banish from her ears. 'It's Grandma!'

Lucy's breath caught in her throat making it difficult for her to speak for a moment. 'Is Grandma all right, Mama?'

Much to Lucy's relief her mother nodded. 'Yes, at least for time being. The doctor has just given her a dose of laudanum, so she should sleep for a while soon. She's asking to see you though. Can you spare a moment before you set off for Chatterton Court?'

Lucy's heart skipped a beat. 'Yes, of course I can.' She touched her mother's shoulder and leaned in to plant a soft kiss on her cheek. 'If you like I shan't go. I'll stay here.'

'No, most definitely not. Your grandma was insistent on you going to the house today. You know how much she approves of your friendship with Archie.'

Lucy nodded. She did know that indeed. Archie had a way with her grandmother that few others had, apart from her step father, Nathaniel Knight. He'd been so good to her since she'd found out her true parentage and afterwards had arranged for her to have elocution lessons and to learn French so she had become a proper lady indeed. It was a far cry from her days in the East End of London, though she had never forgotten her roots. So much so that Aunt Bessie was still a regular visitor to the house and treated like royalty whenever she arrived.

With her heartbeat thudding in her ears, Lucy made her way up the stairs, along the corridor and to her grandmother's bedroom. Where once she had been the formidable Lady Fanshaw to Lucy, she was now Grandmother, or at times, Grandma. She'd been living at the home of her daughter and son in law at Meadowcroft Manor ever since she'd taken ill and Lucy had been so glad of it too as she needed their help. She would have hated the thought of the elderly woman living in that huge, rambling house all alone except for her staff.

Tapping softly on the door, she heard her grandmother's feeble voice cry out, 'Please enter.'

The door was opened wide by a young maid called Hetty, who smiled shyly at her. Hetty reminded her of herself at the same age, so vulnerable and willing to please those in authority above her, yet having a strong spirit at times.

'You may leave the room for a few minutes, Hetty,' Lucy said softly. Normally she would have allowed the girl to stay but it was evident from the conversation with her mother that Grandmother had something she wanted to say.

When the maid had departed, Lucy rushed to the bed and sat in the plush velour covered seat beside it and took her grandmother's pale, gnarled hand. It reminded her of a piece of crepe paper, the skin was that fine and beneath it she could clearly see the blue of her veins.

Grandma was dressed in a white cotton gown that came up to her neck in a ruffled affect, it had a fine cornflower blue ribbon threaded through it and small delicate flowers embroidered on the bodice. To be fair, young Hetty did a good job of looking after her grandmother, she kept the bedding and the nightclothes spotlessly clean, though she guessed her grandmother's condition would be difficult for the staff in the laundry room with so many changes of both sheets and nightgowns required in one day.

'Come here, child,' Grandma said. Although she'd lost a lot of weight, her mind was still razor sharp and her blue eyes active and curious, they belied her condition really.

Lucy leaned over the bed. 'Yes, Grandmother, what was it you wanted to say to me?'

Grandma began to cough and Lucy turned to the bedside cabinet and lifting the small glass pitcher, poured water into a cup and passed it to her grandmother. She took a few small sips and settled her head back down on the pillow. And satisfied that the coughing fit had ceased, Lucy breathed a sigh of relief and set the cup back down on the cabinet as her grandmother closed her eyes.

Was she drifting off to asleep? She didn't like to disturb the woman if she was.

She waited a moment but there was nothing from her grandmother save for the rhythmic rise and fall of her chest.

She began to tip toe away thinking whatever it was the woman had to say to her it could wait until later, until she heard the woman say sharply, 'Lucy! I called you here for a very good reason!'

Lucy froze. Oh no, Grandma was about to tell her she wouldn't be of this world much longer, she was sure of it.

'Please forgive me, Grandma, I thought you'd fallen asleep as you needed your rest?'

Grandma's sharp blue eyes darkened. 'There's plenty of time for me to rest when I'm dead.'

Lucy rushed back over to the bed, then falling to her knees and splaying herself over the bed she began to sob. 'I never want to lose you ever, you've been so kind to me. I shall send word to Archie that I'm not going there this afternoon as I wish to stay with you.'

Grandma stroked Lucy's hair and then as if she was showing too much affection, which she wasn't really known for, she cleared her throat. 'You'll do no such thing! Now get on to your feet and sit yourself back down in that chair and listen to what I have to say with no interruptions, please!'

Lucy nodded and peered at her grandmother through glassy eyes. 'Yes, Grandma,' she sniffed.

'Use your handkerchief and blow your nose, please. No more snivelling.'

Lucy smiled through her tears and she took a seat beside the woman.

'I called you here today not to prevent you from going to see your long time good friend, Archibald Pomfrey, who I still think of as Archie Ledbetter, but to tell you I have a proposition for you!'

'A proposition, Grandma?' Whatever could she mean? Lucy had been convinced the woman was on her death bed but from the spirit she was now exhibiting, that didn't appear to be the case at all.

'I'd like you to become my companion again like you did when you first came here all those years ago.'

'But I don't understand, Grandma.'

'No, well, you wouldn't. I'd like to take a trip overseas. I know I don't have long to go. And no, I'm not about to croak it at any moment, but the doctor says fresh air would do me good and I've always longed to go to Italy and maybe one or two other places. And I'd like you to accompany me. What do you say?'

Grandmother waited in anticipation as she studied Lucy's face for an answer.

'I'd love to go overseas with you, but what if you were to take ill? Your constitution is somewhat delicate.'

'I won't lie to you, you're far too astute for that, but we would take a nurse with us and also a maid. I have spoken at length to Doctor Hamley about this and he agrees that some sun and a change of scenery might do me more good than kicking the bucket and curling up my toes in this house!' Then there was a glint in her eyes and she began to roar with laughter which made Lucy laugh too.

Dear Grandmother, she was one of a kind.

Lucy leaned over and took her grandmother's hand in her own. 'If that is what you wish then I shall be pleased to accompany you on your trip. How long did you have in mind?'

Grandma's face took on a serious expression. 'However long I have left to live, I suppose.'

A tear coursed Lucy's cheek as she held her grandmother's fragile hand to her face as she nodded in agreement.

***

Archie noticed the carriage taking the long sweep of the drive as it came to park up outside the house. The last carriage to arrive had been a couple of weeks ago when his Uncle Walter had arrived with his new wife, Amelie. Archie had thought the man would remain a bachelor forever but on a hunting trip, the man had made the acquaintance of a young widow and there'd been no stopping him after that. In truth, it was what had started him thinking about settling down himself. He didn't want to be a single man for as long as his uncle had been. And, although he didn't wish to marry immediately, for there needed to be a decent period of courtship, he did want to make his intentions known for he and Lucy had been more than friends to one another this past few months.

His heart beat increased as he longed to dash out to meet her but one of the servants had beat him to it. As his butler, Baxter, opened the door and announced Miss Harper's arrival, he took pleasure in seeing her excited manner as she came bustling through the door, her cheeks flushed, her brown eyes sparkling and her hair slightly messed up as she handed both bonnet and cape to an awaiting maid.

'Lucy, my dear,' he said, stepping forward to kiss her hand and lead her further into the room. 'You look perished, come and sit by the fire.'

It was early spring but there was still a nip in the air at times.

'Archie,' she said breathlessly. 'I'm so pleased to see you.'

He gestured for her to take an arm chair near the fire while he took the one opposite, and as she sat stretching out her fingers near the flames he marvelled at her beauty. She'd always been a beauty to him and he'd been spellbound from the first time he'd seen her stood on a wooden crate washing the dishes at The Horse and Harness coaching inn when she was the tender age of twelve and he just ten years old. He'd seemed to have caught up with her age wise over the years and she'd turned into quite the young lady. She'd lost her East End accent after all those elocution lessons and so had he, though both were aware of lapsing back into it at times if they were extremely excitable or distressed.

'It's been far too long,' he said looking into her eyes.

'But you were at my home only last month.'

He chuckled. 'I know I was but it seems so long ago now.'

At that point, Baxter returned. 'Cook is asking if you and Miss Harper might like some refreshment, sir?'

Archie returned his gaze to Lucy. 'Would you like to take a pot of tea with me? And some sandwiches maybe?'

Lucy nodded. 'That would be lovely.'

Archie looked at Baxter who seemed to be caught in a stoop of not knowing whether to bow his head or stand up straight at that point. 'If Cook could prepare a pot of Indian tea for us with some of her infamous cheese and pickle sandwiches, with a slice each of her fruit cake, that would be marvellous,' he enthused, raising his voice a notch so the old man could hear him.

Baxter nodded, then straightened himself up, to walk with a stiffened, shuffling gate towards the door. When he was out of earshot, Archie said, 'By rights, Mr Baxter should be retired at his age but I haven't the heart to let him go. He was so kind to me as young lad struggling in Whitechapel.'

Lucy nodded. 'You did a very kind thing taking him on to live with you when you took over your father's property.'

'To be truthful, I needed someone to give me some guidance on how to become accustomed to living the high life. I mean, I had my Uncle Walter of course but this was my very own house and scary for a young lad of ten years old, who'd come from the squalor of the East End. You of all people understand that?'

'I do indeed, it's almost as if we've reinvented ourselves I suppose.'

'But we're still the same people deep down, aren't we?'

She nodded, then chewed on her bottom lip, was something troubling her? He wondered. But then, she smiled and changed the subject and then they were chattering away as old friends often do, comfortable in each other's company and safe with one another.

After they'd taken high tea, Archie suggested a stroll in the grounds. 'I would have suggested we go riding together,' he said, 'but I can see the way you're dressed so beautifully that this just wouldn't be the right time?'

She smiled. 'Some other time, maybe?' She quirked a quizzical eyebrow at him.

'What? Or should I say, pardon?'

'I just have the impression that you've brought me here to tell me something or other?'

He paused a moment and took her hand, 'And what makes you say that?'

'Because you've been so quiet during this walk, thoughtful somehow?'

She stared past him into the distance almost as though there was someone approaching behind him.

'What are you thinking, Lucy?'

All at once her brown eyes looked guarded and serious. 'I get these feelings sometimes, almost like premonitions I suppose. I don't profess to be a psychic or anything, but maybe it's a kind of intuition…'

He frowned. 'Intuition?'

'Yes, I have a feeling that what you are about to say is going to come between us.'

He shook his head vehemently, 'Oh, no, no, you misunderstand, my dear sweet, Lucy!' Then he was on his knees in front of her and kissing her gloved hand. 'I brought you here to tell you that I wish to marry you!'

There was a long silence and as he dared to look up through his floppy fringe he saw that she was smiling at him. 'Oh, Archie, I didn't expect you to say those words, please rise to your feet.'

He stood unsteadily at first and then produced a small black velvet box from the inside pocket of his jacket as she stood there in awe. He opened the box to reveal a blue sparkling sapphire ring surrounded by miniature diamonds.

'It's beautiful,' she gasped.

'It's yours if you'd like to marry me,' he said and then for the first time, noticed that she had tears in her eyes. 'What's the matter? Don't you wish to marry me?'

She swallowed hard. 'It's not that, it's the timing, it's all wrong.'

'Wrong? But how is that?'

'Let's go back to the house and I'll explain things to you.'

Chapter Two

1874

"The Inheritance"

Archie stood in awe staring at Chatterton Court, the large imposing house with its turreted towers, as his Uncle Walter placed a reassuring hand on his shoulder. Inheriting a house as well as an ancestral name at the tender age of ten years old, greatly overwhelmed him. He swallowed. 'Is this really all mine?'

'Yes, but everything is in trust for you at the moment until you reach the age of twenty-one,' his uncle said in a serious tone.

He looked up at the man who had a big beaming smile on his face. 'What does that really mean though, Uncle Walter? I don't really understand.' One moment he had been an urchin on the streets of London, then reunited with his uncle and now all this!

'I know it's a lot to take in, Archie. Let me put things simply for you: someday all this shall be yours and yours alone but right now a responsible adult has been appointed to oversee the estate. You shall be given a monthly allowance for food and clothing whilst the bills will be paid by the appointed person with money from the estate.'

Archie scratched his head. 'I think I understand, Uncle Walter.' He frowned.

'You looked worried, Archie. What's wrong?'

'Nothing, it's just that I'm frightened of having to live there all on my own. I have no idea how to run any house never mind one this size!'

'You won't be alone in this, don't worry. You shall have an army of servants to help you and the adult concerned shall appoint a tutor for you too and a housekeeper and even…'

'A butler?' asked Archie, hopefully.

His uncle grinned. 'Any particular butler in mind?' He asked knowingly.

'Mr Baxter. I should like to ask him to come here to work for me as I trust him.'

'I'm sure that can be arranged but don't hold your hopes up too high as Mr Baxter might like working where he is for now.'

'I know he likes it there well enough but he did once tell me he wouldn't mind a change and a move out of the city when we were having one of our little chats…'

Archie's mind drifted off for a moment as he recalled how friendly Mr Baxter had been towards him when he'd first started delivering hot pies baked by Bessie Harper to the house where the man resided and worked as butler. That house was a four storey one and would in truth fit into a corner of this one.

'Anything else concerning you, Archie?'

Archie nodded. 'Yes, who will the appointed adult be? I hope it will be someone I like.'

Walter chuckled. 'Oh it is and you do!'

Archie frowned again. 'Who then?'

'It's me! I was a friend of the family and I was named as the appointed person in your father's will.'

Archie let out a breath of relief. 'I'm so relieved about that, Uncle Walter. Why do you think my father never asked to see me or mentioned me as his son when he was alive?'

Walter cleared his throat as if faced with a difficult dilemma to explain to Archie. 'It wasn't all that clear cut you see, Archie. Number one, you were born out of wedlock and number two, your father was already married to someone else, so if it were to become common knowledge, it would have hurt a lot of people and caused such outrage.'

'I think I understand...' he said sadly. But he didn't really, all he remembered was how poor they'd been living in a small run down house in the East End of London. A man had visited late at night when his mother thought he was fast asleep but he couldn't be sure who that fellow was. When he grew up he was going to make sure that his children knew who he was and he wouldn't be ashamed of them either. What hurt him most was that he was his parents' dirty little secret and that made him feel unclean.

'Come on,' Walter said kindly as if he could sense Archie was on the verge of tears. 'I've got the key, we'll go inside and take a look before the solicitor arrives. Then we can tell you a little more of how this will all work.'

Presently a shiny black carriage drew up outside the house and then a gentleman Archie recognised from the day of the party he held at Huntingdon Hall, alighted. Mr Peterson, his uncle's lawyer.

The man wore a long black frockcoat, top hat and crisp white shirt with grey cravat at his throat.

Seeing Archie he smiled as he walked towards them carrying a leather briefcase. 'Hello, young man,' he greeted.

Archie smiled nervously. Although Mr Peterson seemed a kindly sort of gentleman, he was aware of the fact that this man held his future in his leather case and that made him concerned.

As they all ascended the steps, a lady with a round face and sparkling blue eyes opened the door for them. 'Hello, I'm Mrs Morgan the housekeeper,' she said. 'Cook has prepared tea for you all in the library. Or would you gentlemen prefer something stronger?'

'Something stronger, please!' Archie asked hopefully, causing both his uncle and Mr Peterson to chuckle.

'Tea should be fine, Mrs Morgan,' Uncle Walter affirmed.

Mrs Morgan had a strange accent that sounded all sing song to Archie's ears. He couldn't make up his mind if her accent was Irish or not but he thought he'd ask his uncle later.

The woman showed them down a long corridor that seemed to go on for ever. It echoed their footsteps as they passed by and Archie wondered who the men and women and even children in the paintings that looked down on him were. Was one of those his father, he wondered?

Finally, Mrs Morgan opened a large wooden door to reveal a room that housed walnut book cases from floor to ceiling. There was a small fire in the grate and Mrs Morgan looked at them and asked, 'Indian or Chinese?'

Indian or Chinese what? Archie wondered. Were they about to meet a new person and had to choose which one?

'Indian for me, please!' Mr Peterson said decisively.

Archie looked at his uncle wishing they could have had that something stronger which probably meant ginger beer, he thought. His uncle looked at him and smiled and then back at the housekeeper. 'Indian will do nicely for both of us too, Mrs Morgan.'

Archie said nothing, but took a seat opposite the two men who were already seated on the plush looking sofa. They began to chat with one another about this and that. Small talk really about the weather, the state of the economy, what was in the newspaper that day and so forth, but still there was no sign of any Indian woman or man or child come to that.

A few minutes later, a maid arrived carrying a tray with a silver teapot and three cups and saucers which she set down on a low table beside them. 'Your Indian tea, gentlemen,' she announced and she bobbed a curtesy before she departed. Archie noticed there was a plate of biscuits on the tray and he longed to reach out for one and take it to his mouth, but realised that would be bad manners. The maid turned back to look at the trio. 'Would you like me to pour for you?' she asked winking at Archie as if she could sense he wanted to get his hands on one of those biscuits.

To his relief, his Uncle said, 'yes'. When the girl had gone, Uncle Walter offered him a biscuit and as they sipped their tea which Archie now realised was the Indian the house keeper had spoken of, and Archie had finished his biscuit, Mr Peterson began. 'Archibald, you realise that you are now inheriting all this property, don't you? And who your father was?'

He swallowed. 'Yes, sir. My father was Richard Pomfrey. Though I never met him, Mr Peterson.'

'Yes, that is correct. Your father was a man of means and a lord as in he was a sir, but not a sir as in how you address your elders, but a sir with a capital S. Sir!'

Archie nodded but he found it so confusing. 'What's the difference then, Mr Peterson?' He hesitated from using the word sir so not as to confuse things even further.

'Well the Sir I mean as in Sir Richard Pomfrey, means that he was very wealthy indeed and owned a lot of land around here, in fact as far as the eye can see down towards the village of Foxbridge. It is an honorary knighted title that has been passed on down through the generations.'

'Cor!' Archie exclaimed as he slipped back into his East End accent with excitement. 'I've seen those knights in those armour thingies in books and such. They rode on horse back and stuff like that.'

Mr Peterson smiled and his uncle stifled a chuckle.

'Yes, something like that, Archie,' Mr Peterson confirmed.

'Now I believe your uncle has told you that you won't be able to inherit everything as in all the family money right away, not until you're twenty-one years old?' Archie nodded. 'And that he is to be a trustee in charge of your inheritance?'

'Yes, sir. I mean Mr Peterson.'

'That's all right. You can still call me sir if you wish but it won't be the same sort of Sir as your father was.' He brushed a hand across his moustache. 'I've brought along the necessary paperwork for your uncle to sign for you. Arrangements are being made for you to have a tutor for time being, but it was your father's wish that you study at Oxford University.'

Archie almost spluttered on his tea. Him going to university!

'You mean a scholar or something like that, sir?'

'Precisely,' Mr Peterson said as he withdrew a paper document from his case and set it down on the table in front of them.

Archie looked at his uncle for confirmation. 'It will be fine, Archie, you'll see. If you are to become a young man of breeding then you need to go to one of the finest educational establishments in England!'

He didn't want to let his uncle or anyone else down for that matter but Oxford University? He'd hardly had any schooling up until now apart from the private tutors his uncle had employed to teach him at Huntingdon Hall.

Recognising that this was quite daunting for him, Mr Peterson spoke. 'Now don't you worry, young man. I know this is scary for you but you won't be expected to go to university without having sufficient knowledge first. There is a local public school a few miles away where you shall have a good education.' Archie smiled as if relieved. 'It's what your father wants for you, it says here right in his will.' He tapped a brown paper envelope beside him. 'Apparently, it's the same school he attended as a boy and so did your half brother. The family name is well known there.' He cleared his throat. 'It's my understanding that your father donated a sizeable sum to the school whilst he was alive, so that should pave the way for you.'

Pave the way for him? What did the man mean by that?

'For time being, you don't need to worry about such matters,' his uncle reassured. 'It shall all be taken care of and you have a couple of week's grace before you begin at Compton Manor School.'

So that was the name of the place! In truth he'd never even heard of it before and he'd have felt more at ease being tutored at home or in a school in Whitechapel where he knew his own class not with a bunch of toffee-nosed kids who hadn't had to work for their keep. You could be sure that none of those would have been forced to clean any chimneys. He just had to speak to Lucy to tell her all about this, she'd never believe it. And, oh, wouldn't that mean that he wouldn't see much of her when he was at school? But then the lawyer said something that made it quite clear he would be separated from everyone and everything he knew for some time yet.

'I need to inform you, Archie, that this type of school is a boarding school…'

Archie blinked as he searched the man's face for clues. 'A boarding school, Mr Peterson. What is that?'

Uncle Walter intervened. 'It's a school where you are expected to live in during term time, Archie.' Noticing the look on his nephew's face, he continued, 'but you will be allowed home for holidays and maybe one or two special occasions.'

Archie felt a lump in his throat as if he might cry but he didn't want to in front of them so he just nodded instead as his eyes glazed over. All of this, the house, the grounds, the money, meant nothing to him if he was to be parted from everything he loved, including his uncle. Why did he have to discover who his father was? And why did the man have to insist he take over everything and go to boarding school and some snotty nosed university?

Uncle Walter touched Archie gently on the shoulder and spoke softly to him. 'It won't be so bad, I promise. I went to a similar boarding school myself. The time will fly by and then you'll leave there ready to take on university and eventually the world...'

***

Lucy had just finished having a lovely lunch in the dining room with her mother, step father and grandmother, when Meg, her personal maid, appeared at the door. She whispered something to the new butler, Fortescue. Grandma had eventually got rid of old Grimes and the housekeeper on Lucy's advice, when she'd discovered a lot of what they'd got up to behind her back. The betrayal by both had run deep.

Fortescue walked over to the table and clearing his voice said, 'Mr Archibald Pomfrey is here to see the mistress.' He glanced in Lucy's direction.

'Are you expecting him?' Mama asked looking surprised.

'No, I wasn't, but I'd like to see him nevertheless.' Lucy tossed her napkin on the table as she looked at them all for confirmation that it was fine with them.

'Very well,' said grandma, 'but please inform him that in future he needs to let us know in advance if he is paying a visit.'

'Thank you, Grandma!' Lucy enthused as she rose from her chair to place a kiss on the elderly lady's cheek.

Grandma pretended she didn't go in for such affection but Lucy knew she secretly liked it from her.

'Take him into the drawing room,' her step father advised.

Lucy nodded and she followed the butler out of the room and into the hallway outside where Archie was stood with his head lowered. There was something wrong she just knew it and she longed to take him into her arms and give him a hug, but as the butler was hovering nearby, she shyly said, 'Hello, Archie. What brings you here today?' He looked up at her as a tear coursed his cheek, unable to speak. 'I tell you what, we'll go into the drawing room.'

'Will you be wanting any refreshment, Miss?' Fortescue asked. If he'd noticed that Archie was upset he wasn't saying so as he waited patiently for an answer.

'Yes, please. If you could arrange for a pitcher of lemonade and a couple of iced finger buns to be sent to us.'

'Yes, miss.' He bowed his head and turned to walk away in the direction of the kitchen.

Lucy took Archie by the arm before anyone had a chance to see how upset he was. She didn't want any of her family or servants to witness his distress as she knew how proud Archie was. He'd hate them to see him this way. What on earth could be upsetting him so?

When they entered the drawing room she closed the door behind him and led him over to the fire place where she took a seat beside him on the sofa and automatically draped her arm around him and cuddled him to her. 'There, there,' she soothed. 'Cry it out whatever it is, Archie, then we'll talk.'

He nodded and then took a huge wracking sob that made his body shudder. She put her hand inside her dress pocket and handed him her cotton handkerchief. 'Wipe your eyes and blow your nose, you'll feel better then.' He did as told and appeared to have composed himself.

She lifted his chin with her thumb and forefinger, so that he brought his glistening eyes to meet with hers. 'Now what's the problem? I want you to share it with me.'

'It's just that I've found out just how big the house is that I told you I was inheriting…'

She blinked. 'So, that's good, isn't it? Why should that upset you?'

'Because my real father left mention in his will that he wants me to attend Oxford University, but first I have to attend his old public school.'

'Yes, but schooling will be good for your future. A good education will take you places in life.'

'I understand that but as it's a public school it means that I have to live there. Oh, Lucy, it means I'll only be allowed home for high days and holidays!' He began to sob again.

'Now, now, it will be hard for you at first but you'll get used to it and think of all those new friends you shall make.'

'I suppose so,' he sniffed. 'I won't be able to see much of you any more though, Lucy.'

'Don't talk daft,' Lucy said. 'I can see you when you come home and maybe I can visit and we can write letters back and forth to one another.' She turned her head away not to show him she had tears in her eyes too as she'd miss the best friend she ever had.

Chapter Three

1885

"An Explanation"

After disrobing and settling themselves back down near the flickering flames of the fire in the hearth in the drawing room, Archie gazed at Lucy as his heart leapt. The flames and the fading light illuminated Lucy's shadow on the wall. She looked so beautiful sat there with her dark curls loose upon her shoulders and a faint rose blush to her cheeks from their earlier walk but he just could not understand her reticence. 'What on earth is it? How is the timing wrong for us? We're both grownups now with money behind us. I'm twenty-one years old and have now officially inherited everything here, all the documentation passing everything over to me has been sorted out. Uncle Walter is no longer required to be my trustee. I am now my own man and I want to give you everything, my darling,' he said with a tone of exasperation.

She swallowed hard, fighting to hold back the tears. 'It's not you, Archie. I care for you so deeply. It's…' she let out the sob she'd been holding back as her shoulders shook from the upset of it all. This was so hard to bear, now of all times. Something that ought to have been such a happy occasion for her.

'What is it then?' his tone was softer now.

'It's grandma,' she sniffed.

'Is she against our union then?'

She shook her head. 'No, she really likes you, Archie, and she approves of our relationship.'

'What is it then?' He threw up his hands as if in despair. What was it that was stopping her from saying a simple 'yes'? This wasn't how he'd imagined his proposal to be. He'd envisioned her almost swooning into his arms like at the end of a romantic novel, saying it was all she'd every yearned for to settle down with the man of her dreams in his beautiful home. He just couldn't fathom her out. Hadn't they been through so much together in Whitechapel as kids?

Was there some other reason she didn't want to marry him? Surely there wasn't someone else, was there?

***

Lucy felt bad as she could sense Archie's frustration, but she had a duty to Grandma. The woman had been through so much, first losing her husband and then her daughter for some years. The kindness she had shown both her and Auntie Bessie held no bounds, for she'd saved Lucy from having to live a life in Whitechapel where her prospects were grim. The best she could hope for was to become married to a man who worked his guts out for a pittance a day and then maybe get saddled with a house load of kids. She'd shivered at the thought of that. Grandma had welcomed her into her home on the pretence of seeking a companion. She'd known all along that Lucy was her granddaughter, but not that her own daughter was still alive.

Lucy let out a long shuddering breath. 'She's dying. Grandma's dying.' There, she'd uttered the words she'd been holding back.

He looked at her for a moment without saying anything at all, she thought he was about to smile, but then he looked confused as he frowned. 'I sympathise, Lucy, I honestly do as your grandmother is a woman is of a certain age but I don't understand why that would stop us from getting together with one another?'

She shook her head as tears threatened to spill down her cheeks. Taking a deep breath, she explained, 'She has asked me to accompany her on an overseas trip to spend her final months visiting the places she has always longed to go and I've already agreed. She wishes for me to become her companion just as I did years ago when I first turned up at the house. She has been so kind to me, Archie. How could I possibly refuse her last wish?'

His frown ironed out and then he was on his knees beside her looking deeply into her eyes and wiping away her tears with the pads of his thumbs. 'I understand, darling. I don't want you to leave if I'm honest, but now you've explained, then I guess it might only be for a few weeks at most.'

She nodded. 'It sounds from what the doctor has told her that is the case.'

He took her hand in his rather larger one and said firmly, 'Then I shall wait, we can always write letters to one another. But I'm worried about you as it sounds to me as if she wants you with her when she passes away.'

She nodded and sniffed. 'I think so, Archie.'

'But why not your mother and Mr Knight. Why you?'

'To be honest, I'm as shocked about this as you are, Archie. All I can think of is that it's because she promised me years ago that she'd like to take me on a trip to Europe.'

He nodded. 'I can't help thinking she'd be better off in her own surroundings though, with all her family and her doctor at hand.'

She smiled. 'I think it's because she longs to go somewhere where she'll feel better in herself and able to visit the places she's never been to before it's too late.'

He squeezed her hand. 'Very well then, I'm happy for you to go as long as we become engaged on your return. I need to pledge my love to you in front of the whole wide world.'

Her eyes sparkled as she replied, 'I'll think about it. Let's discuss it on my return.' He looked hurt and confused for a moment, and then, she was in his arms as they both stood and he brought his lips to hers. He had never kissed her with such passion before and by rights she should have had a chaperone with her, but knowing they were to be parted for who knew how long made her cast her cares away and get swept up in the moment.

Parting would be such sweet sorrow but although he had such deep feelings for her, she had her doubts about them going their separate ways for a time. He'd seemed so shocked when she'd turned down his proposal.

'You'll come and see me off at the quayside when I leave?' she asked.

Archie nodded, but then he stood and stared out of the window and she wondered if there were tears in his eyes like there were in hers.

She blinked and left him to it, finding it difficult to remain in case she broke down and changed her mind.

***

At the quayside, there was a lot of hustle, bustle and noise as people rushed to board the ship as loved ones bade farewell and porters loaded trunks and bags onto the awaiting vessel. Lucy could see the ship's rails lined with rows of passengers ready to wave to loved ones down below. Glancing around, she noticed many people beside her, with distraught expressions on their faces at the thought of their loved ones leaving shore.

Aunt Bessie was there stood beside Lucy's mother and Nathaniel Knight. Bessie was dabbing at her eyes with a handkerchief. 'I shall miss you so,' she sniffed as she planted a kiss on Lucy's dampened cheek as she had been crying herself.

'Now you've got everything, haven't you?' her mother reminded.

'Yes, Hetty has checked and double checked and so has the nurse,' Lucy reassured. She looked into the distance behind her mother in the hope that she'd see Archie as he'd promised to see them off too.

'Come on,' Grandma said forcefully. 'We don't want to be the last on board or to get swept along in a stampede.'

'Can we have five more minutes, please?' She looked at her grandmother for confirmation.

The woman looked as if she was about to relent when Nurse Enid Carmichael came along and tutted. 'No, your grandmother is quite right we need to board now so I can settle her down for the journey as it will be an arduous one.' She lifted her fob watch from her dress to take a peek at the time. 'Her medication is due shortly and we wouldn't want her to suffer now, would we?' She gave Lucy a hard stare which made it difficult for her to object.

With sinking heart, Lucy realised the woman was right, even though she found her very abrupt and bossy at times when it came to her grandmother, she thought she only had the woman's best interests at heart.

'What's the matter?' Hetty whispered as the others spoke amongst themselves to say their final farewells.

'It's Archie, he promised faithfully he would be here to say goodbye…' she sniffed. 'After all we might not see one another for weeks and weeks.'

Hetty nodded and then smiled. 'How about if we board as planned and I'll keep watch from deck for him, if he shows up, perhaps I can take a message to him or he can come onboard just before we set sail?'

'That's a good idea, Hetty. Thank you.' Feeling a little more reassured, Lucy said her farewells where there were lots of hugs and tears and the four of them set foot on the gang plank.

The S. S. Maritime was taking them to France first, then they were going to sail to Spain and finally Italy. Lucy had her doubts about the journey. Would Grandmother withstand the journey? But the nurse was well prepared, she'd brought along several bottles of laudanum and Grandma's other medications. There were also two serving doctors on board the ship so that was a relief. Apparently, Nurse Carmichael had checked this out beforehand.

When they arrived at their cabins, Lucy discovered she had her own and so did Grandma, and next door down was one shared by the nurse and Hetty. Lucy pitied Hetty being in a cabin with Nurse Carmichael as she was so regimented that she realised Hetty would have to keep the place spruced up. But then again, neither of them was really here for rest and relaxation like she and her grandmother were. They were getting paid handsomely for their time, and when Grandma was resting, they'd have a little time for activities about the ship or to visit one or two places on land.

At least they weren't stuck in steerage down below with the masses. Lucy remembered a family who had arrived at the coaching inn who'd travelled that way. The father had explained how dreadful the journey had been with so many people cooped up in the bowels of the ship and the mother had spoken of how her children had been sick for a lot of the journey. Apparently, it had stunk to high heaven of sweat, vomit and urine down there. And the food was no better, just dry hunks of bread, salted slices of meat and a thin measly soup most days—and that's if people could stomach it. Hetty and Nurse Carmichael didn't realise how lucky they were.

Lucy chewed on her bottom lip as she glanced around her cabin, which was sparsely furnished with just a single bed, wardrobe, chair and small table, but it was very clean. She opened the door and stood out on the deck to stare down below at the quay. In the distance, she saw Hetty who appeared to be searching the faces of the people who pushed past her to board the ship for fear of missing it. Lucy's heartbeat began to mount as she saw a coach suddenly draw up and a young man alighting from it, she couldn't make out his face, but it could be Archie. Was it him? She brought her hand to her forehead to shade her eyes from the sun, but then her heart plummeted to the ocean as she noticed the man stood there, waiting for a young lady and two, no three young children, that followed behind her. They were a young family waiting to board the ship and it appeared they'd only just arrived in the nick of time.

She began to wave frantically to Hetty. There was no chance the girl would hear her in amongst all the noise and the hooting of the ship's horn and the grey puffs of steam emanating from its funnel indicating it was time to depart. What if she lost her chance to board the ship all because she wanted her to wait for Archie, who obviously was not going to arrive? What would they do then? Grandma needed the young maid as much as she needed her nurse to care for her.

Hetty suddenly turned without even seeing Lucy and as if she'd had the same thought, she boarded the ship behind the young family, waiting patiently in her place, the last passenger to set foot on the gangplank.

A lump grew in Lucy's throat as she fought to hold back the tears. He'll be here now any moment at least to wave from the quayside and he might not even see me, but I'll see him, she thought. But as she waited as the ship finally pulled out of port, the hard realisation hit her full force.

He wasn't coming.

Archie hadn't even bothered to see her off and that really hurt. She returned to her cabin in amongst the jostling crowds who had stood on deck to wave to their friends, families and loved ones, through a blur of unshed tears. She pushed open her cabin door and threw herself on her bed and wept into her pillow, no longer interested in the merriment that was taking place outside as it seemed to reflect the opposite image of her own misery. Archie was making it obvious that he no longer cared as she had turned down his proposal in favour of a trip overseas with her grandmother. She hadn't even agreed to an engagement when they returned as he'd suggested, just a promise given they'd discuss it when she got back to England.

***

Archie stood by the side of the dusty road with his coach driver. Why on earth did there have to be trouble with one of the coach wheels right now? A little further down the rickety road, he'd heard a strange noise and the coach had veered out of control until the experienced driver had brought it to a halt and calmed the horses down.

'I'm afraid we're not going any further at the moment, sir,' he said, removing his hat and scratching his partially bald pate. He looked at Archie for confirmation as if to see if he thought the same thing.

'It would happen today of all days, Jenkins,' Archie said as he shook his head.

'My apologies for that, sir.'

'It's not your fault. I know you always make thorough checks of the vehicle and horses beforehand; this road is particularly bad.'

Jenkins let out a long breath as if relieved he wasn't being blamed for this. He sat on a large protruding rock near the roadside and Archie sat cross legged on the grass beside him. 'Best I can think of, sir, is for us to leave the coach and lead both horses to a coaching inn I know that's a couple of miles down the road. If we make it there, you never know you might be able to pay someone from the inn to take you there—that way you might just make it in time.'

Archie nodded. What other choice did he have? Though if they made it there, time would be tight and that was only if he could find someone to immediately help him. But what else could he do and the longer they sat and thought about it the less chance he'd have of getting to the quayside to see Lucy off. He drew out his gold watch from his pocket and peered at it. 'Yes, we'll do as you suggest. If you can unharness the horses and we'll ride them bareback to the inn.'

Jenkins nodded. 'We're taking a chance leaving the coach, mind you,' he said stroking his chin as if having second thoughts. 'Do you want to wait with it while I see if I can get help?'

'No, the coach is the least of my concerns, if it gets stripped of its wheels or taken all together, that's a chance I'll have to take.'

Jenkins nodded. 'Very well, sir,' he said rising to his feet and Archie following suit.

Lucy meant more to Archie than his damn coach any day. Objects were replaceable, people were not.

They made their way on horseback to the inn, thankfully Jenkins remembered the route well as he'd taken it several times over the years for the Pomfrey family when they'd taken trips overseas, though it had been about fifteen or sixteen years he reckoned since he'd last taken that particular route.

'Not much further now, sir,' he said as they approached a cross in the road which pointed one way to Malverton where the inn was situated and the other towards the quay itself. Archie hesitated a moment as he felt his trusty charge beneath him, he was taking a risk he knew but Jenkins had told him that Atticus was the strongest and fittest of both horses.

'You go on ahead to the inn for help with the coach, Jenkins. I'll ride over to the quayside instead, it's the quickest way of doing this, believe me…'

'But, sir, you're not familiar with the area and the terrain is very steep and rocky…' his coachman said but his voice trailed into thin air as, with a whinny, the black horse Archie was riding took off at speed.

He just hoped and prayed he'd get to his love in time before she left the country. He brought his thighs hard against the stallion's flanks as he pulled on the reins, making him gallop even faster. Archie didn't even have any time to think about his safety as all he cared about was Lucy and taking her into his arms one more time. In the distance, he noticed the fields giving way to a few small houses and he realised that this was the village of Crandon that Jenkins had told him about as they had both intended stopping off there on the way back from seeing Lucy off. He tried slowing the horse down as he usually did with his own horse, Casper, by pulling back on the reins. It appeared to be working but then a horse and cart clattered on by and the man on top of it started shouting in a shrill voice, 'Bring out your rag and old bone!' Atticus suddenly startled and reared up on his hind legs. As Archie had no saddle or stirrups beneath him, just a blanket, he fell onto the cobbled ground and hit his head.

As the world spun on its axis, his last thought was, 'I never got to say goodbye…' as everything faded to black.

Chapter Four

1874

"The New School"

Archie gulped as the coach passed through the wrought iron archway and over the cobbled driveway leading to Compton Manor School for Boys.

'Yes, Archie, young man,' said Uncle Walter as he sat opposite him with a glint of mischief in his eyes, 'this is the very same school your father before you attended and his father before him.'

Archie nodded, unsure whether to be impressed or not. 'Did you go here too, Uncle Walter?'

His uncle's face reddened. 'Er, no. My father had the money to send me here, well I did actually attend for a term but...'

'But what?'

'Look, let's just say that it wasn't for me. My father took me out of here and enrolled me in a lesser known establishment but I was happy there.' He tapped the side of his nose with his index finger, making Archie wonder what on earth could have happened. It didn't exactly sit right with him that his uncle had left the school, yet was insistent on sending him here if he didn't like it himself. He was about to say something when the coach drew up outside the entrance where several boys in a similar uniform to himself of top hat, tails, funny shaped white collars and thin black ties milled around. Some had large trunks beside them and there appeared to be a group of older boys who were directing them to where they needed to be.

His uncle looked at him as if realising how frightening and intimidating this was for him. He of all people would and should understand. 'Don't worry, Archie. You will be fine. A lot has changed since my day. After all, I was here about twenty years ago. There's a different headmaster now, old Fellows retired a few years ago. My word I could tell you a few tales about him!' He appeared to be reminiscing, and then realising he needed to keep Archie on side, said, 'But those will keep for some other time. Come along, we'll go inside and I'll settle you in. But I won't hang around too long as you'll need to get to the dorm with the other lads.'

Archie sighed. 'Can't I come back home with you, please, Uncle Walter?'

Walter looked at him for a moment as if he was about to relent. Then he patted Archie's arm. 'No, I'm afraid you can't. We have to follow your father's will to the letter if you are to inherit his fortune eventually. He has stipulated that this is the school you are to attend. Now don't worry, you'll be back home with me for half term, it will soon fly by. In any case, you can't possibly turn around and go back home now after being fitted out for your new school uniform, and Cook went to all that trouble to send you away with all your favourite cakes she baked especially for you. I'm sure she's packed a chocolate sponge cake in the hamper! Chin up, young man!'

A tear coursed Archie's cheek that not even the thought of one of Cook's chocolate cakes could prevent from falling. He sniffed and swallowed and forced a smile. Whatever happened to him now could not possibly be as bad as when he was kidnapped by evil Bill Brackley and forced up searing hot chimney breasts in fancy houses in Whitechapel. He decided to remember that if he ever hit any hard times here at the school.

As if reading his mind, his uncle said, 'Don't forget you're a tough cookie, Archie. Half of those namby pamby sorts in there won't have weathered what you've been through. Doubt if they could cope with it. But you, sir, have shown mettle. Not only did you cope with working for that chimney sweep but you were a trouper and you helped young Lucy and Bobby to escape too. That proves you have spirit and pluck, my boy. Think of that sometime when you need to.'

Archie nodded, and feeling so much better, followed his uncle out of the coach. As he stood on the gravel gazing up at the large daunting grey building before him, which was really an old manor house, hence the name, he suddenly thought, 'For the first time in my life I am a proper school boy, a scholar at last.'

They were met at the entrance by a man in a black robe who was directing people towards the hall. 'There's a general meeting in there,' he said, 'for all new comers and their families. What's the young chap's name?'

Archie was about to answer for himself when his uncle said, 'Archibald Led...er I mean Pomfrey.'

The man raised a silver brow. 'Well, well, young man,' he smiled broadly and offered his hand for Archie to shake.

Archie took it tentatively, quite surprised at the man's reaction to the name.

'Yes, we've had a few generations of Pomfreys at this school. The last being William of course. I never knew he had another relation though? Are you his son or his cousin?'

Archie cleared his throat and he felt quite embarrassed as a queue of people had built up behind him as they waited patiently to enter the school. 'No, sir. I'm his brother.'

For a moment, the man looked slightly flustered. 'Oh, I didn't realise he had a younger brother, there must be quite some years between you both. I was so sorry to hear of his sad passing. Another old Compton Manor School ex pupil taken too soon...' Then as if to change the subject, he added, 'If you both make your way along the corridor and the main hall is the last door on the left. I'm Mr Crowther, by the way, head of religious studies.'

They both thanked the man and entered the large arched entrance. Once inside, Archie turned towards Uncle Walter and asked, 'Why did Mr Crowther seem so surprised that William Pomfrey was my brother?'

'It's not common knowledge, Archie,' he whispered. 'I'd keep it to myself if I were you, well until someone raises the subject.'

He nodded, feeling now though as if he was slightly soiled. His mother kept it a secret all those years ago and now he felt as though he was being forced to keep a secret himself. In any case, if his real father wanted to send him to the same school where all the Pomfrey men had been schooled then he could hardly agree to keep it a secret could he, with a name like Pomfrey?

As if realising that Archie was perplexed, his uncle added, 'Well, why don't you just tell them you are a relation but not go into any detail, if that's easier for you?'

Archie nodded but he didn't like it one little bit.

***

When all the buzz had settled down in the hall as the murmurings and scraping of wooden chairs on the highly polished floor had died away as people took their seats, a man, who Archie didn't recognise, stood on the stage at the front of the room. Behind him was a long row of seats where men of all ages wearing similar attire to what Mr Crowther wore, sat patiently. The man at the podium looked slightly older than the others. Archie noticed his white neatly trimmed side burns and full cheeks. His ruddy complexion made him appear as either he'd been drinking port wine, as Uncle Walter looked like that after doing so, or as if he'd been in front of a roaring fire, Archie decided. Maybe both.

The man wore a funny black square thing on his head with a tassel attached to it. 'What's that on his head?' he whispered behind his hand to his uncle.

'It's called a mortar board hat,' Walter said. 'He's the headmaster here but sometimes the teachers wear them too.'

Archie nodded and watched as he waited for the man to speak.

'Good morning, everyone!' He greeted as his black voluminous gown appeared to billow out around him. 'I am Mr Criddlington, the headmaster of this fine establishment. When I've finished speaking, I'll introduce you to the staff and explain which departments they belong to, then we shall all have a welcome cup of tea and other refreshments. And then, following that, I shall read out a list of all the boys and the forms they shall be attending. Then they'll be taken away by their form tutors. Their luggage shall be taken by the porter to the dormitory and Matron shall later show them where their beds are allocated et cetera.' He cleared his throat, 'Meanwhile we shall sing the hymn 'Jerusalem…''

For the first time, Archie noticed a young man sat behind a black grand piano as he played the introduction and they joined in. It was a hymn that Archie was familiar with. *And did those feet in ancient times walk upon England's mountains green…*

Then there was a prayer and after that, Mr Criddlington told the boys about the history of the school. Some of the lads were openly yawning, which Archie found quite rude especially as they didn't cover their mouths with their hands when doing so. Uncle Walter had taught him that, but after a while, he found he was no longer listening himself as the headmaster droned on and on. It seemed never ending.

His uncle shot him a stern look. 'Sit up straight, Archie!' he reprimanded.

Archie did as told. It was unusual for Uncle Walter to tell him off like that but he guessed he wanted him to start off on the right foot.

Following that long introduction, Archie was taken away with a group of other boys by their form tutor, Mr Pennyworth. He looked at the boys surrounding him and felt totally out of his depth after they spoke of their lifestyles, none of them would have been forced up a sooty chimney or made to sleep on bare floorboards beneath a dirty coal sack! Of that he was certain. But he made an effort to join in as they chattered amongst themselves as "Old Penny" as one of them referred to the master, swept them along the corridors at a swift pace. They walked quickly around the corner to a seeming never ending corridor of wooden floors and tiled walls, where paintings and old photographs of former pupils and teachers hung in frames, looking down at him in distain. Archie gulped as some of those teachers faces looked very stern indeed.

He felt a nudge to his elbow and then looked across to see the boy beside him, as they had been instructed to walk two a breast, offering him a toffee.

Archie smiled and took it from the lad who had a shock of red hair and a smattering of freckles. 'I'm Daniel Carruthers,' he introduced.

Archie nodded. 'I'm Archie Pomfrey,' Archie replied.

Daniel smiled at him making Archie feel more at ease, but the rest of the boys all seemed to know one another and he felt a little left out as they seemed to act as if he wasn't one of them, which puzzled him. How did they already know one another?

Finally, Mr Pennyworth stopped outside a room and opening the door, said, 'This will be your form room, boys. Go in and claim a desk each and then you are to stick to that desk for the remainder of term. I will have no moving around, understood?'

All fifteen boys looked at him as if waiting for a command and then they stampeded into the room. Unfortunately for Archie, he was the last through the door and ended up with the wooden desk at the front of the room, which he didn't much care for because now he would be right in Old Penny's view!

He glanced over his shoulder to see Daniel behind him, who smiled, so that wasn't so bad, but he so wished he could sit beside him. Instead, there was a large lad sat there who wore specs.

When the group had settled in, Mr Pennyworth asked them all to introduce themselves one by one and to say a little about who they were and where they came from. As Archie was first, he had no idea at all what he should say, so after a moment of contemplation, he began, 'My name is Archibald and I live a few miles away from this school. I didn't know I would be attending here until a few weeks ago.'

Mr Pennyworth who was seated at his desk, peered over his round framed specs, 'Oh, and why was that?'

'It was stipulated in my father's will, sir!'

'I see.' Then as if making a connection the teacher cleared his throat. 'Are you telling me then your father was Sir Richard Pomfrey?'

Oh no! He'd gone and done the very thing his uncle had warned him not to, given away who his father was. 'Y…yes, sir…'

There was a deathly hush in the classroom and Archie didn't understand what it meant? Did they all know his father? Who he was?

'I see,' said Mr Pennyworth, breaking the silence. 'Your father was a very generous benefactor to this school and from my, er, understanding, he has left us a sizeable sum in his will and for that we are extremely grateful.' He smiled as if pleased about the fact, but Archie got the impression that he was shocked that he was the man's son.

'So, then Archibald, tell us what you like to do then? No doubt you like horse riding like your father?'

'No, sir. I mean I don't know, sir.'

Someone giggled at the back of the class.

'What do you mean you don't know? Surely your father, as he kept horses, took you out on them?'

'I never met my father, sir…'

The laughter died down.

'I'm sorry, I don't quite understand?' Old Penny continued. His eyebrows knitting together in confusion.

Oh dear, he was getting himself in some very deep water indeed and feared now he'd have to explain the circumstances of his birth, thankfully, as if realising this, Daniel interrupted. 'I don't much like riding either, sir.'

Archie let out a breath of relief.

'And why is that, Carruthers?'

'Because I once fell from a horse and hit my head, sir. I haven't been back on one since, even though Father keeps asking me to do so.'

Old Penny shook his head and rolled his eyes, then turned his attention on to someone else. Archie turned behind him to look at Daniel who winked at him, it was then he realised that the boy had been lying to help him out.

When all the boys had introduced themselves and Mr Pennyworth had told them all that would be expected of them at the school, there was a knock at the door.

'That'll be Matron Bagley,' he announced. 'She'll take you to the dormitory and will give you blankets and pillows to make up your own beds.'

Archie heard a few loud groans coming from the back of the classroom. He guessed those boys were a bit upset at having to do something for themselves when they were used to being waited on, hand, foot and finger at home.

'Please enter!' Penny shouted at the door.

Archie stared in amazement as a large rotund woman, who wore a long blue dress, over which she sported a pristine white frilled apron, entered the room. On her head was a frilled mobcap in the same pristine white condition as her apron. Her sharp beady eyes scanned the room. 'I'm Matron Bagley and I'll be keeping you boys in shape whilst you board here, understood?'

The noise had faded away. It was as if each boy who had earlier been showing off was now in complete awe of this woman as if afraid, even more so than of Old Penny, who seemed quite easy going by nature, and of the head himself.

'I have a few rules you'll need to abide by,' she sniffed. 'Keep those and we shall all get along famously. You shall rise at 6 o'clock every morning and use the facilities on waking. But I must stress that you keep them clean, I don't want to find any puddles of urine around the place. Then you shall wash with soap and water, especially your ears and neck!' She held up a finger. 'Then you shall dress. All night attire is to be put away in the wardrobes provided by the side of your beds, if anything needs washing then it is to go in the large wooden tubs at the end of the dorm. Beds are to be made up before breakfast, nothing is to be left hanging around the dorm. All books and other items are to be placed in the wooden boxes beneath your beds. No food is to be left in the dorm as it encourages rats!'

Rats! Yikes!

Archie felt a shiver run the length of his spine as he recalled some of the rats he'd seen around the Whitechapel area which were as large as small cats. It hadn't even occurred to him that they might have a problem at a fancy place like this where the boys' fathers paid an exorbitant amount of money each term.

Someone at the back shouted, 'Please Mrs Bagley, what are we do then with the tucker we've brought with us?'

'I was just coming to that.' She smiled for the first time. 'I'd like all hampers brought to my quarters where they shall be kept under lock and key, I have a large pantry there to keep things cool too. Your treats from home will be doled out to you sporadically. If for example, you have given your masters no problem all week and completed your course work, then on a Friday evening and over the weekend too, you shall be allowed to have a couple of items, which you will need to sign for. I shall keep an inventory of these things. One thing I cannot abide is gluttony! It's one of the seven deadly sins!'

What on earth was a deadly sin? Surely someone wouldn't drop dead from eating one too many pies or an extra slice of chocolate cake?

'Now then, there is another issue I must address and that is bedwetting!' continued Matron.

Archie felt his face flame. He wasn't usually a bedwetter unless under stress, was she talking to him? But he released a breath as he realised, she was addressing everyone.

'It's quite natural in a group of this size to have a couple of bedwetters, which is something everyone grows out of eventually. However, I'd appreciate if those boys who are bedwetters could come to me before this evening, then I can supply them with rubber under sheets.'

She went quiet for a moment as she scanned the room with her beady eyes as if to wait for a couple of boys to raise their hands to admit to their bedwetting, but of course none did. 'Come along now!' she clapped her hands, 'there's nothing to be ashamed of...'

Still silence. So she said, 'Well if you are one of *those* boys come to my office before tonight and speak to me discretely so we can arrange something. I don't want any of the beds, as we have some new mattresses this term, to become sodden with urine. That would be most unfortunate.' She sniffed loudly as if imaging the odour beneath her nostrils.

Oh dear, what was he to do now? Did he 'fess up and have one of those rubber sheets or go without and hope he didn't have an accident? He decided to keep quiet for time being. No way did he want to embarrass himself in front of those other boys.

When the boys had finished unpacking their belongings and each had made up their beds, Archie went for a stroll on the landing. He stood gazing out of the arched leaded window as the carriages below were beginning to pull away from the drive. Fathers and sons were being parted from one another, though in this case, he was being parted from his Uncle Walter. He drew in a breath as he spotted the man boarding his own carriage and knocked the window with his knuckles in the vain hope that his uncle would look up to see him standing there, waving goodbye. But he didn't. Archie's heart plummeted as fat tears rolled down his cheeks. He had never felt so abandoned in all his life, apart from when his mother had died of course. He drew a handkerchief from his trouser pocket and wiped his tears and sniffed. It wouldn't do to show any kind of weakness in this place, of that he was sure.

Chapter Five

1885

"Kindness of a Stranger"

As the ship powered on, Lucy decided she now needed to pull herself together and stop thinking about Archie. She was here for her grandmother and if she brooded too long over why he hadn't shown up to see her off earlier, then she could spoil the whole trip. There may have been many reasons for his failure to show up.

She closed her eyes for a moment as the warm breeze blew on her face, ruffling her hair.

'Miss, are you okay?' She turned to see Hetty by her side with a concerned look on her face.

Swallowing down her sadness she turned towards the girl, forcing a smile. 'Yes, I'm fine, Hetty. Thank you for asking. How is my grandmother?'

'She's settled into her quarters well, Miss. I've left her resting on the bed. Nurse Carmichael has just given her ladyship her medication, so I think she'll have a little snooze before too long. She told me to go and get some fresh air as I won't be needed for some time.'

'Oh good,' Lucy said brightening up. 'Shall we see if we can find some refreshment? I heard some passengers mention they were heading off for tea and cake in the dining room.'

'Yes, please, Miss,' Hetty said smiling. Lucy felt like linking arms with the girl but she realised it wasn't the done thing as she was brought away with them as domestic help not as a friend or relative. Hetty as Grandma's maid and Enid Carmichael as her nurse, for the sake of her grandmother's welfare, needed to be close at hand and were fortunate to travel first class themselves not down below with everyone else of their own class.

It wasn't too long before they followed the swell of excited passengers headed towards an open set of doors. They had found the dining room. Lucy gazed around in awe at the crystal chandeliers, heavy velvet embossed wall paper and the tables neatly set with white linen table cloths, expensive looking china crockery and silver stands with all manner of fancy cakes adorning them. There were a couple of waiters in attendance ready to lead people over to the tables and to check their cabin room numbers in the book on a small counter in front of them. Lucy and Hetty were fortunate to be assigned one of the last remaining tables in the room. A notice on the wall read that high tea was taken between the hours of three and five o'clock each afternoon and it was served in two separate sittings. As it was minutes to three, they were fortunate that they wouldn't have to wait another hour in the bustling queue that was now forming outside.

As they took their seats, Hetty said, 'We timed that right, Miss!'

'We certainly did,' Lucy answered. Her stomach was beginning to settle down. Earlier she had thought that maybe she had developed some sort of motion sickness but now she realised it was her anxiety about Archie not turning up that had caused her queasy stomach. She was just about to lift the menu to peruse it when she heard someone clear their throat. She glanced up to see a man stood near the table in a long grey jacket with matching trousers, white shirt and black cravat at his throat. His silver brocade waistcoat set off his attire and he looked quite the dandy. His slick coal-black hair was neatly smoothed down, there wasn't a hair out of place. His appearance was quite a contrast to Archie's, who often swept his floppy fringe from out of his eyes or left his cravat slightly askew at times.

'Yes?' she said, meeting the man's dark eyes.

'Excuse me, ladies,' he said with a charming smile and a strange accent. 'I was hoping to take tea this afternoon but, gee, you both beat me to the last table here and I was wondering if I might share it with you?'

Affronted by the man's nerve, Lucy was about to refuse the stranger's request, when Hetty looked at her with pleading eyes. She was obviously quite smitten and, in any case, what harm could it possibly do? She let out a long breath of annoyance which she half hoped he'd hear and change his mind. She glanced around the dining room, it was busy and he would need to wait another hour to be served after queuing up outside. 'Very well.' She gestured with her white gloved hand for him to sit down.

'Splendid!' He enthused as he took a seat and settled himself beside them. 'Thank you, ladies. And might I say I am honoured to be in such charming company on my journey home!'

At that point, before Lucy could ask where home was, a waitress appeared beside them. She wore a long black damask dress, pristine white apron and white lace cap. She held a small notepad and pencil in her hand ready to take their order.

Lucy perused the menu as the waitress patiently waited. 'I think I'll have the afternoon special please, the selection of sandwiches, miniature assorted cakes and a pot of tea, please.' She looked across at Hetty. 'And the same for you?'

Hetty nodded and smiled and then went back to staring at the stranger with the same faraway look in her eyes that she'd had when she'd first set eyes on him.

'And you, sir?' the waitress asked.

'I'll have the same, please, but with coffee instead of tea. I've drunk so much tea during my time in Great Britain that I feel I am swimming in the stuff. You seem to drink it all day long there!' he chuckled.

The waitress smiled and nodded and then departed to put in their order.

Lucy was about to ask the stranger where he was from when Hetty blurted out, 'Where are you going home to then?'

'New York, miss,' he replied.

'New York?' Lucy arched a brow. 'But you're on the wrong ship, sir. This is going to France.'

'Surely not? I've met other passengers on here who are also going to New York. Is it you who is on the wrong ship, honey bunch?'

Lucy exchanged glances with Hetty, whose face flushed bright red. 'Didn't your grandmother explain, Miss?' she asked.

Lucy slowly shook her head feeling very foolish indeed. This was a transatlantic voyage not one just across the English Channel—she had been misled. Feeling affronted, she stood and with her chin jutting out and tears in her eyes said, 'I can't believe I've been deceived like this…and by my own grandmother of all people!' She made to turn away to leave the room, but then the man took her hand. He'd already annoyed her and now she felt shown up by him. Though none of this was his fault.

'Please seat yourself,' he said gently guiding her back to her seat. 'Have a little think about this while we partake of the tea. You'll do yourself no favours if you storm into your grandmother's cabin right now…'

'She'll be asleep anyhow after her medicine,' Hetty said soberly.

Lucy nodded. 'I suppose you're both right.' Reluctantly, she seated herself down once again, then found a large silk handkerchief being pressed into her hand by the man. 'Not the best way to introduce myself, but I'm Sheldon Harper Brown, ma'am. Please take this to dry your eyes and I promise you'll feel a lot better after you've left here rested than if you go all guns blazing out of here right now.' He took his seat once again.

She nodded, genuinely touched by his kindness. Wiping her eyes, she sniffed. 'Thank you, Mr Brown. I am *Miss* Lucy Fanshaw and this is our maid, Hetty.' She emphasised the word "Miss" as she found it odd that he referred to her as "Ma'am".

Hetty beamed at him but Sheldon only had eyes for Lucy. 'Please call me Sheldon,' he said smiling. And for the first time since Archie hadn't shown up to see her off from the quayside, Lucy felt her disappointment ebbing away.

By the time the sandwiches and pots of tea and coffee had arrived, Lucy felt like she'd known Sheldon much longer than ten minutes. He really was the most charming man she'd ever met, such good company, but she became aware that they were almost excluding Hetty from their chit chat, so Lucy began to bring her into the conversation whenever she could and then they both smiled as Hetty related tales of when she used to work at another grand house and the scandalous goings on there.

'It's not much like that where I live,' Sheldon chuckled, 'oh, we have servants and such but I think our class system is somewhat different. America is the land of opportunity and you shall see that when you get there, Lucy. In fact, you may never want to return home when you find out all it has to offer...' he patted her hand as he held her gaze a little too long. 'And you would be welcome to call at my home any time. I shall make a point of writing down my address before I leave the ship.'

When Sheldon left the table to speak to a nearby waitress, Hetty whispered, 'He's awfully nice, ain't he, Miss?'

Lucy nodded, all the while keeping her gaze on Sheldon as he spoke animatedly to the waitress. His shoulders filled his jacket so well, he really was a sharp-dressed man and she'd never met anyone like him before.

He returned to the table with a glint in his eyes. 'I've just asked if we might have a bottle of champagne delivered to the table,' he enthused.

Lucy's eyes widened. 'But I've only ever sipped sherry when it's been a special occasion like someone's birthday, or at the New Year,' she said, 'never champagne!'

'Well this is a special occasion as I've just met you both,' he said with a smile.

In no time at all, a waiter arrived at the table presenting a bottle of champagne for inspection in his white gloved hands. Sheldon studied the label. 'That will do nicely, thank you!' He placed some coinage in the man's hand. 'And this is for you,' he said. The waiter smiled and nodded. Then he uncorked the bottle which made a loud popping noise, causing customers heads to turn in their direction.

The waiter poured a glass and passed it to Sheldon for him to taste. He took a sip and then nodding at him, allowed him to pour three glasses.

'Cor!' Hetty said as her eyes widened. 'This will be me first real glass of champagne. Are you sure, sir, that one is for me?'

Sheldon chuckled. 'Yes, of course it is, young lady. Enjoy it. Champagne and life were both meant to be enjoyed. That's my motto at any rate!'

By Lucy's second glass of champagne, she had almost forgotten how annoyed she was with her grandmother for deceiving her like that. As if he could read her mind, Sheldon leaned in towards her and said, 'I shouldn't be too annoyed with the old dear, you know.'

'And why do you say that?' She blinked several times.

'Well, from what Hetty's just said about her it sounds as if the heavy sedation she's taking might be fogging her mind.'

Lucy smiled and blew out a long breath. 'You know, I hadn't thought of that before.'

'Is she in a lot of pain then?'

'Well, no, not exactly..."

Sheldon lifted a brow. 'Oh? I assumed as you mentioned this would be her last trip away that she's at death's door. Pardon me for saying so and making that assumption.'

What he said hit a chord with her and was making her question things. 'Yes, it is odd, we only have her doctor's word for how she is doing.'

'Do you think then that maybe the doctor is giving her unnecessary medication to make her sleep?'

'I suppose it is possible. I might have a word with her nurse.'

'Yes, by all means do that,' he said smiling. 'But think about bringing her to visit my doctor in New York when you arrive. He's a very forward-thinking gentleman indeed. A fine physician.'

Lucy nodded. But what concerned her was the fact, if grandmother's doctor was keeping her sedated unnecessarily, why would that be so? She decided to forget about it for now and just enjoy the moment but later she would have a word with Nurse Carmichael.

'Ooh miss, me 'ead is spinnin'' Hetty said.

Lucy observed the girl across the table whose colour now looked lily white and her countenance seemed a little shaky. Lucy made to rise to go over to the girl.

'Perhaps you'd better return to your cabin,' Sheldon suggested. 'Would you like me to escort you there?'

Hetty shook her head. 'No thanks. I will do as you suggest though, Sir. I'm not accustomed to this high living.' She let out a loud hic.

'I'll be over shortly to check on you,' Lucy added as the girl stood and trembling, made her way across the tea room.

'She'll be all right,' Sheldon assured. 'I'll tell you what, I'll order a pot of coffee, shall I?'

Lucy nodded gratefully; she didn't want to end up in the same state as Hetty. Though the girl had gulped her drinks down instead of sipping them. Poor thing. With the rocking of the ship and all, there seemed to be a bit of a storm whipping up.

Sheldon raised a gloved hand to summon a passing waitress to order the coffee, and then, he gazed at Lucy.

'What brought you to England?' she asked.

'I've been there on business,' he said, then he smiled a smile that lit up his grey-blue eyes. 'I'm an author you see. I'm in the middle of writing a book.'

'Oh!' Lucy was immediately interested. 'I don't think I've ever met a proper author before. Well only once, there was one staying at the inn where I worked as a young girl.'

He quirked a brow. 'How was that? I mean you seem a lady of breeding, how come you worked at an inn?'

'It's a long story which I might tell you some day but I'd like to find out about you and your book first.' She folded her hands beneath her chin as her elbows rested on the table as she listened intently.

'Well, to be truthful the living conditions of people in the East End of London have always interested me…'

'Really? That's where I once lived, in the Whitechapel area.'

He straightened up. 'Remarkable! That's where I was staying. I wanted to see what it was like living there. I stayed at several places like guest houses, doss houses and even the workhouse! That was an experience I can tell you, ma'am!'

She nodded. 'And what did you discover about the place?'

'Oh, that there are all sorts there. A lot are good folk who have fallen on hard times, even the working girls. That the area is overcrowded…'

'Did you ever stay at somewhere called The Horse and Harness? It's a coaching inn.'

He shook his head. 'No, but I may have called in there for a drink once, the name sounds kind of familiar. Is that the inn you used to work at?'

'Yes. I was a kitchen maid there for some time. It was hard work though.'

He took her hand across the table and pressed it to his lips whilst gazing deeply into her eyes. 'It's hard to believe that these lily-white soft hands could have once worked at that particular establishment.'

She smiled. 'Well they did but they weren't so lily-white back then, believe me. I was up at the crack of dawn lighting fires and sometimes even scrubbing floors, though my main job was to help the cook, Cassie, in the kitchen.'

'Please tell me what happened to you and how things changed, Lucy,' he pleaded, looking at her with avid interest. 'How did you end up changing your fortune in life?'

She spent the next half hour explaining how she'd been found by her Aunt Bessie abandoned on a bench at Itchy Park and she was eventually reunited with her real mother who came from a wealthy family.

'That's truly amazing!' His eyes lit up. 'I have an idea, would you mind if I interviewed you for inclusion in my book, Lucy? I'm writing a follow up.'

Her eyes widened. 'Oh, I don't really know about that…'

He pleaded with her. 'It would make a great addendum to the book as I'm writing about the British class system and the haves opposed to the have nots but your particular story seems to buck the trend as you've experienced both sides of the blanket as it were. For my first book I went undercover but the second deals more in the statistics of poverty. What makes someone poor, that sort of thing.'

'May I think about it?' she asked. 'It does all sound rather interesting though…'

'Of course. This passage will take about two weeks to cross the sea to New York so we shall have plenty of time to get to know one another. It may take a little less if the crossing is particularly good though.'

Lucy's heart began to race. 'Thank you,' she said and then she continued, 'you have been very good company, Sheldon. I had better return to my cabin now and check on both my grandmother and Hetty.'

He stood and walked towards her to help draw out her chair as she stood, and for a moment they were in very close proximity towards one another as he steadied her. She experienced something she had never felt before as he touched her, not even with Archie, a frisson of excitement was pounding in her veins as her cheeks flamed red hot. This stranger had lit a flame inside her that was beginning to burn so strong.

Chapter Six

1874

"A Bullying Brute"

'Come on, out of your beds!' Matron's shrill voice pierced Archie's brain. He'd had a restless first night and so had some of the other boys as he'd heard one or two whimpering during the night or whispering to one another. He, himself, had been afraid to get out of bed for fear of being reprimanded, but he'd been vaguely aware of a few getting up to use the lavatory and being escorted back to their beds by Matron. It seemed as if he'd never drift off to sleep and when he finally had, now he was being rudely awoken.

He sat up in his bed and stretched his arms, turning his head to see Carruthers gazing at him from the next bed over. 'How'd you sleep?' he asked.

'Not so good,' Archie admitted, yawning and rubbing both eyes. 'It's so strange being here.'

Carruthers nodded. 'Some of these boys are used to this as they were here last term but I wasn't.'

'Oh, I see,' said Archie, rising and throwing his legs over the side of the bed, his striped flannel night gown badly creased from all his tossing and turning during the long, never ending night before. 'That explains how they know one another then.' No wonder he felt so out of things, but at least he now understood why they appeared so cliquey with one another.

'Yes.' Carruthers ran his hands through his shock of red hair which appeared to be sprouting in all directions after being in bed. 'Come on,' he said with a note of urgency to his voice, 'we'd better get a move on or Matron won't be best pleased with us.' Archie nodded. 'And watch out for him, over there, Ashcroft.'

Archie's eyes were drawn to a tall, well-built lad who was already dressed in school uniform as he stood near the door as if inspecting the boys as they passed by, clipping one or two of them across their heads for dawdling. He had a cocky sort of swagger about him that reminded him of Smithy from the coaching inn. 'Who is he, then?' Archie asked.

'He's the head of Blue House, which is what we are part of here in this wing of the school. He's in the sixth form. Apparently, according to my cousin, he's a whizz at rugger! No one can catch him. Best rugby player in the school but you don't want to get on the wrong side of him. He has several younger boys under his wing from each form, who he uses as spies!'

'Spies?' Archie blinked then swallowed hard.

Carruthers lowered his voice a notch. 'Yes. They'll pretend to be your friend but tell on you if you break any rules, so watch out for those or you'll get punished by the teachers, or even worse, those lot will mete out their own punishment.'

Archie frowned. 'Who are *they* then?'

'I don't rightly know, but best to treat everyone like a spy until you know better,' he added as if he was an expert on covert matters at the school.

Archie was about to reply, when Matron marched right up to them. 'Didn't you boys listen to what I told you?' she said sharply. Her eyes seemed to be bulging out of her head and her top lip quivered.

'N..no, I mean yes, Mrs Bagley.' Archie trembled.

Matron yanked his ear, forcing him to stand, so much so that it hurt. 'One little lesson you'll learn today is to listen first time around, now off to the washroom and scrub your face and neck, and don't forget to clean those lugholes, I could grow a crop of potatoes in those! Now get dressed, my lad.' She let go of him causing him to stumble backwards on to the bed and then she turned her gaze towards Carruthers, who immediately backed away and both boys bade a hasty retreat towards the corridor and the washroom.

After washing and dressing, the boys made their way to the dining hall for breakfast by following the horde there. The rest of them seemed familiar with the daily routine at the school. The tables were long and bare wood, set out for each class with a prefect at the head of each table. Archie was relieved to discover that Ashcroft wasn't assigned to their table, but a boy of about the same age as the bully was. His name was Samuel Parker Moore. He sat at the head of the table in a chair that seemed slightly higher than theirs so he could peer at them as they ate which made Archie feel very uncomfortable indeed. Was he doing something wrong? He removed his elbows from the table as his uncle had told him he shouldn't rest them there, it was bad manners. It was as if the lad was just waiting for one of them to make a mistake. By his side was a leather-bound small notepad and pencil and Archie guessed he would use that to record various misdemeanours. Oh, how he wished he was back home with his uncle. He'd be dining with him right about now and then he'd go into the garden most probably to see Mr Featherstone the gardener before his tutor arrived. Mid-morning, Cook would often call him into the kitchen for a cup of tea and a scone or some other tasty treat afterwards to share with her and Polly. Here, he felt very small indeed.

A bowl of thick oatmeal was placed down in front of him which he found hard to digest as it was so thick and lumpy. It was highly salted too which he disliked as he preferred sugar or honey on his. He ate it as best as he could, spooning the thick congealed gloop into his mouth, he'd had worse when he'd lived with Bill Brackley, so he supposed he should be grateful. He drank his glass of milk in one go to get rid of the horrible gunk in his mouth, only to realise that when he thought breakfast was over, it wasn't! A plate containing a kipper and piece of bread and butter was then plonked before him. He didn't mind kippers though but his stomach felt full and he'd already finished his drink, but he was relieved to see a middle aged waitress heading towards their table with an earthenware jug containing milk to top up any empty glasses. She winked at Archie as she passed by and topped up his glass. He smiled at her, then diverted his gaze as Samuel was staring at him. He liked the look of her though as she was the first real friendly member of staff he'd encountered at the school.

When breakfast was finished, the headmaster announced that it was time to get to their classrooms and Archie's class followed Old Penny to the room they were in just yesterday. Thankfully, the lad who yesterday had seated himself next to Carruthers had decided to claim Archie's desk at the front without even asking him if he minded. The switching of desks suited Archie though as he was able to sit beside his new friend behind now. It was then Archie realised that maybe Mr Pennyworth had organised the desk move as the other lad wore spectacles and might have had problems seeing the blackboard.

'Right, boys,' Mr Pennyworth said, 'I want you to make a note of your weekly time table in an exercise book. It shall remain the same all week and every week. You'll find all you need in your desks.' He waited patiently as the boys lifted their desk lids to extract pencils, fountain pens and exercise books. 'Now then, straight after breakfast every morning you are to begin lessons. I do allow a few minutes flexibility for you to use the latrines after breakfast before coming here, but I do expect you by your desks at eight o'clock sharp!' He tapped his thin willow cane lightly on the desk in front of him. 'Now then,' he said as if to make a point, 'I don't use this often, but I do from time to time if someone misbehaves!' He whacked away at thin air with his cane so that it made a strange whishing sound which made Archie tremble. Up until now, Old Penny had seemed affable enough, but as if to exert his authority, he cracked his cane down heavily on his desk which appeared to make all the boys startle in their seats. He raised his voice and Archie thought he heard one of the boys whisper 'Oh, Mummy!' behind him. Old Penny had seemed unthreatening yesterday when he'd first introduced himself, Archie had no idea the man could be this stern. 'Now then, jot this down…' He said in a lighter tone so that he sounded kindly once more.

'Monday morning first thing, will be a double period of mathematics...' Daniel Carruthers groaned beside him, as the teacher carried on, 'Followed by a single period of geography. After luncheon you shall have another period of geography...' on and on he went, speaking so quickly that Archie had a problem writing it all down. He glanced across at Carruthers who seemed to be a whizz at writing quickly and his penmanship was highly legible too.

Half way through the morning, the boys were given a break outside in the grounds and as groups of boys congregated around the building, Archie peered far into the distance at the playing fields and further on in the direction of the woods. There was supposed to be a secret lake somewhere, his uncle had told him and he wouldn't mind taking the chance to take a peek at that. But if he went right now he might get in trouble if he wasn't back in time and old Penny had warned them not to roam too far.

'Look at that!' Carruthers exclaimed. He pointed to a disturbance across the school yard.

Archie turned his head to see a fight had broken out between two of the boys in their form who were going for one another in a moment of fury as fists were flying and the boys toppled onto the floor, rolling about, each trying to get on top of the other. Archie was hoping to have a look to see what it was all about but then Ashcroft and Samuel Moore arrived to break them up. The crowd that had gathered began to disperse when they arrived, probably for fear of being in their firing line. Ashcroft held up one of the boys by his collar much to the amusement of his classmates.

'Well, what do we have here then?' Ashcroft said gruffly as the boy dangled before him like a piece of meat on the hook at the market place. 'Answer me boy, name and form number?'

'Widmore. Class 1A2, sir!'

Ashcroft laughed and cruelly let him go so he fell to the floor in an undignified heap. It must have hurt like hell Archie thought and he was fast starting to hate Ashcroft, the big bully, he reminded him of Bill Brackley. People like him loved to wield their power over others, particularly younger and more vulnerable people. Ashcroft wouldn't have known about Archie's dealings with that man, nor what Archie himself was capable of. He'd learned a lot on those mean streets of Whitechapel.

One day I'll sort him out—you'll see if I don't! Archie fisted his hands at his side and gritted his teeth. If there was one thing he couldn't stand it was someone who exploited the weakness they saw in others.

When Ashcroft and Moore had departed leaving the boys stunned, their faces agog at what had just happened, Archie went over to attend to the lad. No one else was bothering to check on him. 'Are you all right?' he asked helping him to his feet as the other boys turned and walked away.

It was the lad who had taken his desk. The boy searched the ground for his spectacles, and quickly retrieved them. 'Yes, I'm all right, I'm used to being picked on. I was more interested in finding these as I don't want to lose them, I'm blind as a bat without them.'

'Is that why Old Penny put you in my seat so you can see the blackboard better?'

The boy nodded and smiled. 'I hoped you wouldn't mind as I can see you and Carruthers are quite pally!'

'No, I didn't mind at all, but we have an opening for a new friend, if you'd like to join us?'

The boy slipped his spectacles back on and smiled broadly at Archie. 'I should say so! Thank you!'

After that, Walter Widmore, or Wally as he liked to be called, became firm friends with Archie and Carruthers and they formed their own little army to protect themselves from the other boys and bullies like Ashcroft.

***

Archie had been at school for a few weeks before he received a letter from Lucy. Trembling, after picking it up from Matron's office, he made his way to the dorm. The other boys had just gone to get changed for P. E. but he was ahead of them as he'd already got into his gear.

He sat on his bed and read:

My dearest Archie,

I hope you're settling in well at your new school?

Here, at Meadowcroft Manor, all has been going so well. I've been spending lots of time with Mama and Mr Knight of course. It's strange sometimes to think she is my mother as she looks so young and beautiful, yet I suppose she is still young as she was youthful when she fell pregnant with me. Mama says we have a lot of time to make up for, she keeps planning little outings here, there and everywhere as little treats for me as if to make up for things she feels I have missed out on over the years but to be truthful, Aunt Bessie gave me a good life. Last month, Mama took me to the opera to see La Boehme and next week we're off to the ballet. Imagine me, Lucy Harper, a simple little kitchen maid as I was, going to such grand places and now being known as Miss Lucy Fanshaw? My name has officially been changed by deed poll. There was some talk to begin with whether I should take the surname Knight as it's Mama's married name but as Mr Knight isn't really my father, with some discussion, Fanshaw, Grandma's name, was chosen in the end. I'd have been happy to stick with Harper as Bessie has been so kind to me but when I protested about keeping the name, Grandma explained that by taking my mother's maiden name it would please my mother so much and do a lot to salve her guilt at having abandoned me as a baby. Still, I spoke about it with Bessie and she doesn't mind. She's been asking about you, and I believe your Uncle Walter is arranging to have some of her pies delivered for you and your friends to the school soon at his own expense! Isn't that nice of him?

I miss you so much and hope you're settling in at the school. I keep imagining that maybe you and the other boys get up at the stroke of midnight for a thrilling feast from your hampers! I also imagine you playing rugby for the school. Tell me, am I thinking along the right lines?

I was thinking that when you return home for the holidays that maybe you could come here for tea, if you like. Oh, Archie it would be so good to see you.

Waiting in expectation for a reply.

Your friend always,

Lucy.

Archie let out a long shuddering sigh and then a tear trickled down his cheek. Lucy wasn't right at all, there were no jolly midnight feasts with the other boys because mainly they ignored him except for his new friends, Wally and Carruthers. And Matron would never allow them to have a midnight feast, and even if they could arrange one, they had to sign for their own food and it was only allowed at specific times as she kept the hampers safely under lock and key. And there was no rugby for him at the moment. He'd watched the older boys play it a few times and found he enjoyed doing so as a spectator sport, but no one allowed the younger boys a go at the game. Life for the main part here was quite miserable for him at the moment, but he couldn't tell Lucy that in his reply as he didn't want to worry her. But at least he did have two allies here, Wally and Carruthers. They were his best mates. The thing they all had in common was that they stood out from the rest of the non-descript lads who all acted pretty much the same here—as if they had a plum in their mouths. Wally was a little overweight and quite myopic without his specs so that made him a target to get picked on. Carruthers red hair and freckles got him mocked at, and he, Archie Ledbetter now Pomfrey, amused the boys with the fact he'd never even met his own father. He was a figure of fun and at the moment they were leaving him well alone but he realised that wouldn't last much longer if he didn't win them over soon.

Chapter Seven

1885

"Worries about Grandma"

'Grandmother,' Lucy said softly when the elderly woman had awoken and was sitting up in her bed as Nurse Carmichael went off to sort out her medication for the afternoon, 'why did you not tell me it is America we are off to and not the Continent as you'd first informed me?'

Her grandmother smiled. 'Didn't I tell you, child? I thought I had. Please forgive me as my medicine makes my mind hazy sometimes.'

Lucy sat in the chair beside the bed and took her grandmother's fragile hand in her own. When the nurse had left the berth, she took her chance, 'But why do you need all this medication if it's making you sleepy? What is it for exactly?'

Grandma groaned and shook her head. 'I don't rightly now, the doctor put me on it initially as I was feeling a bit run down but now, he says it will keep the pain away.'

'Oh?' Lucy thought for a moment then said, 'what sort of a pain was it you were experiencing, anyhow?'

'In my back, but the medicine really helps as I haven't got any pain left now, you see. But he has indicated that it will make my last days easier.'

Lucy nodded. 'Yes, I do understand but when we get to New York I'd like you to get a second opinion for me.'

Grandma's eyes widened. 'Do you really think that's necessary, Lucy? I trust my own doctor.'

Lucy patted her hand. 'I know you do but doctors do sometimes get things wrong. I've met a nice American gentleman in the tea room. He lives in New York and says he knows someone who will look you over.'

Grandma raised her silver eyebrows in a quizzical fashion. 'Is that how you found out we are sailing for New York?'

'Yes, and it came as quite a shock to me at first, let me tell you. I was a bit upset already, especially as Archie didn't even show up to wave goodbye before we left…but now I can see this will be the opportunity of a life time for me.'

'I'm glad you feel that way. And I will see that physician you mentioned,' Grandma said in a reassuring tone which pleased Lucy greatly.

'Good,' Lucy said standing and brushing the creases out of her gown, 'but whatever you do, do not mention this to Nurse Carmichael, we'll make out we are just visiting Sheldon at his home and escape from there without her knowledge. Understood?'

'My lips are sealed,' Grandma said, resting her head back on her pillow. It didn't seem right to Lucy that the woman seemed to need so much rest and would be sedated yet again by the nurse when she already seemed so tired anyhow.

'Thank you,' Lucy said, lowering her head to kiss her grandmother's sallow cheek. 'I'll speak to you later after you're up and dressed, maybe we can go for a stroll on deck and take some sea air together?'

Her grandmother nodded and closed her eyes as she drifted back off to sleep. Lucy was finding this most disturbing and she doubted whether the woman would be able to join her for that stroll on deck after all. As she left the berth and quietly closed the door behind herself, she caught sight of Nurse Carmichael hurrying towards her with a small black leather bag in one hand and a folded blanket in the other. The way she was pursing her lips, she was obviously a woman on a mission. Lucy walked towards her and said, 'I know you're busy but can I have a quick word with you, please?'

The nurse came to an abrupt halt and glared at Lucy as if she had no right to do such a thing when she was busy going about her business. 'Very well,' she said with a resigned sigh. 'What is it you want?'

'It's about my g…grandmother.'

'Yes?' Nurse Carmichael blinked several times.

'Why is she so drowsy all the time? It doesn't seem right to me.'

The nurse snorted with derision before replying, 'Doctor Hamley has prescribed the appropriate medication for your grandmother as she needs it. Without it, she would be in severe pain. But of course, it does have the side effect of making her sleepier than usual. Now then, does that answer your question?'

Lucy nodded. 'I do understand that, but might we try a little experiment to see if my grandmother could leave off the medication for a day or two to see if the pain returns or not? After all, if it doesn't, then she might not require it any longer.'

'Most certainly not!' The nurse huffed out a breath of indignation. 'I have been employed to nurse your grandmother and follow doctor's orders. I do not experiment on any of my patients and I'll hear no more of this nonsense!'

Oh dear! Now she'd gone and upset the woman. Maybe she would have been wise to remain silent on the issue for now, at least until they reached New York and she could make an appointment for Grandma to be examined by Sheldon's own physician. Then if he thought the medication was unnecessary, she would have something to back up her idea and might convince the nurse to think differently.

Nurse Carmichael's cheeks appeared to bulge with fury and Lucy thought the woman looked as if she was about to burst, so to calm the situation she said, 'Very well, I understand. You know best, I shall speak no more on the matter.'

The woman said nothing, just turned her back on Lucy and made for Lady Fanshaw's berth. Lucy was about to return to her own cabin when Hetty came running towards her in a flap, holding on to the hem of her dress with one hand as if afraid she'd trip over it and the other hand keeping her straw bonnet in place. 'Miss, I noticed you speaking to the nurse just now!' she said, slightly out of breath as she drew up beside her. 'There's something I wanted to tell you...'

'Yes?'

'It's your grandmother, I think she's addicted to that bloomin' medicine Nurse Carmichael is giving her.'

Lucy frowned. 'And why do you say that?'

'Well, I just went to her cabin a while ago to look for you and she was crying out for it.'

'Oh dear,' Lucy said solemnly. 'I do have concerns about that medication myself and as it's laudanum, I know for a fact it is addictive. I was hoping the nurse would take her off it for a day or two to see if my grandmother really needs it but now in light of what you've just told me, it seems an unlikely prospect.'

'Not only that,' Hetty said, 'I think we need to keep an eye on Nurse Carmichael as maybe she's giving your grandmother a little too much of the stuff, as don't forget, it makes work easier for her if your grandmother's sleeping most of the time. She can do what the heck she likes then with her spare time.'

Lucy honestly hadn't considered that fact. 'Hmmm,' she said thoughtfully chewing on her bottom lip, 'Perhaps you're right, Hetty. I think one of us needs to be around whenever Nurse Carmichael dishes out my grandmother's medication. I've noticed she gives her a spoonful of the medication first thing in the morning at about 8 o'clock, then midday, then about four o'clock as it is now, actually I've delayed her a little so maybe that's why she's so cross. Then she administers the final dose at about eight o'clock at night.'

'I think you're wrong there, if you don't mind me saying so,' Hetty said sombrely.

Lucy raised an inquisitive brow. 'No, I assure you, those are the correct timings.'

'No, what I mean is, they might be the right times, but I've noticed her, back at the big house, slipping into your grandmother's bedroom in the middle of the night when most folk are asleep. I've only noticed it because I've got thirsty once or twice and gone downstairs to the kitchen at about midnight. She hasn't seen me on either occasion, but when I've glanced up the stairs there she was, entering Lady Fanshaw's bedroom.'

Lucy gasped. 'Are you sure?'

Hetty spoke animatedly. 'Positive. So maybe she's giving her an extra dose or two during the night. I think it's odd meself as the lady is a very sound sleeper, so I doubt she's been calling out for her. It also makes sense why I'm always having to change her bed linen as she keeps having little accidents. If the lady is sleeping heavily maybe she can't rouse herself to use the facilities, if you know what I mean?'

Lucy nodded gravely. She did know indeed. 'I was present when the doctor first prescribed Grandma's medication and I specifically remember him saying she was to have just four small spoons of it a day, and then only if necessary, so maybe she is being overdosed and becoming addicted to the medicine. We'll take it in turns to watch tonight. If you can keep a look out tonight after the nurse leaves Grandma's cabin after the eight o'clock dose say until midnight, I'll take over for most of the night.'

'I don't mind doing that, Miss, but that will be a long time for you to stand guard, over eight hours?'

'Not really. I shall sleep in my grandmother's cabin, there's a small curtained off side room where her gowns are kept with a chaise longue, I shall sleep on that. That way I can have my sleep but I shall hear if anyone else enters the room.'

'Good thinking, Miss,' Hetty said, her eyes gleaming.

'I tell you what,' Lucy said, 'it might be an idea for you to sleep in there for the first four hours too rather than you popping back and forth, and then I'll take over at midnight.'

'Very well, Miss. By the way...' she said, changing the subject, 'would you like to bump into that American gentleman again?'

Lucy thought about the prospect for all of two seconds before replying, 'You know, I think I would, Hetty. I need to see him again in any case to let him know that my grandmother has agreed to be examined by his physician once we arrive in New York.'

Hetty beamed. 'And what did your grandmother say when you told her you had no idea that's where we were headed until you met him?'

'She apologised and blamed the laudanum for making her confused that she hadn't mentioned it to me.'

Hetty nodded. 'I can see how that might happen.'

Lucy chewed her bottom lip. There were more reasons than one as to why she should try to find out whether her grandmother needed that medication or not.

***

Later, as Lucy took a stroll on deck before dinner, a cool breeze had whipped up as the sea water became choppy and she felt the sea spray hitting her face. Stumbling to one side, she was about to reach out for the rail when a strong pair of hands stabilised her. She turned to see Sheldon stood beside her as her heart gave a little flutter of admiration for him.

'Oh, thank you so much,' she whispered. 'Things seem to be getting a little rough.' She smoothed down a strand of hair that had flown in her face.

'Yes, as we head out over the Atlantic Ocean it can get like this when we can't see any land for days and days…'

'You sound like a seasoned traveller?'

He smiled. 'I suppose I am, Ma'am, though I don't cross the Atlantic that much, it's more within my own country that I travel.'

Lucy found it amusing that Sheldon referred to her as "Ma'am" and not "Miss" as she would be referred to as an unmarried lady at home. 'I've heard that America is such a big country compared to Great Britain,' she said.

He nodded and offered her his arm so they could stroll together, she took it, feeling proud to accept. 'Oh, it is, but I have to say I love your country. Gee whizz, it's so quaint and the people, I find rather eccentric at times!' He exclaimed looking down at her.

She looked up at him and took in how handsome he really was, his finely chiselled masculine jaw, his dark eyes twinkling mischievously as he spoke with an accent and tone she could listen to forever. His neat dark hair was well coiffed, and she suspected, smoothed down by use of pomade or some other similar product that kept it so well-groomed looking. And the way he filled his jacket made him appear all man to her. She felt protected in his company and her heart swelled to be beside him.

She giggled. 'I hope you don't mean me, Mr Brown?'

'No, not you, Ma'am. You seem quite modern and forward thinking to me. A typical English rose, might I say!'

'You certainly know how to charm someone,' she said.

'No,' he said looking deep into her eyes, 'I mean it. It's not a throwaway comment, you are a lovely looking lady.'

She found herself blushing as she turned away for a moment, but secretly, she was pleased. She was totally at ease in his company as the conversation flowed, it was like being in the company of an old trusted friend, who just happened to be handsome and attentive.

'Lucy,' he said stopping in his tracks for a moment, 'you will absolutely love New York. As the ship will approach the harbour you'll see the Statue of Lady Liberty. It's a large statue of a lady holding a torch aloft. The attraction won't be open to the public until sometime next year but you'll see it and will be amazed by it.'

'Really? What does the statue represent, freedom?' She was eager to learn more about this new and vibrant sounding place.

'She stands in Upper New York Bay and yes, she represents a universal symbol of freedom. It was a French gentleman named, Edouard de Laboulaye, who first proposed the idea of a monument for America in 1865. Then ten years or so later, a sculptor was commissioned to design a large statue. It was to be completed in 1876 to commemorate the centennial of the American Declaration of Independence. The Statue was named "Liberty Enlightening the World" and was a joint effort between the countries of America and France. It was agreed that the Americans build the pedestal beneath the statue, and the French people were responsible for the statue and its assembly here in America. Sadly, though, there was a lack of funds.'

She frowned, puzzled for a moment. 'You mean the money ran out?'

'Yes.' Slowly, he nodded his head. 'That's about the sum of it. There was a lack of finance on both sides of the Atlantic Ocean. Both countries though ended up employing different methods to raise funds. In France, for example, they raised money by having a lottery and employing public fees, et cetera, while in America theatrical shows, art exhibitions, auctions and even prize fights, were arranged.'

'That's so interesting,' Lucy said thoughtfully.

'Yes, basically, the statue is a beacon of hope to the world and it's the first thing people see when they enter New York harbour as she welcomes them to America the free.'

'I know a few people who have emigrated to America, or the New World as they called it.'

He nodded. 'Which parts did they go to?'

'The ones I know converted to the Mormon faith and ended up going to a place…hang on there's some sort of lake in the name.'

'Yes, I know where you mean, Great Salt Lake in Utah.'

Lucy nodded. 'But what I don't understand,' she said, 'is why people give up everything to travel so far away from their friends and families? The people I knew were a young married couple who had been converted by listening to Mormon missionaries who preached on the streets, then they got baptised into the faith. Now they might never see their brothers and sisters or parents ever again, or friends come to that.'

Sheldon stroked his chin. 'Possibly, but you can't make that sort of assumption as it's possible that they might either return to Great Britain some day or their families might follow them out there if they're having a better life than at home. The world is becoming a smaller place and any chance to get away from hardship should be taken in my opinion.'

'That's true. It was hard going when I lived in Whitechapel. Many wanted to escape from there.'

'Yes, the trouble with Whitechapel is the overcrowding. I'd never seen so many people crammed into one small area in my life. Remember I said I'd like to interview you for my book?'

'I've not forgotten,' she said thoughtfully.

'How about I interview you tomorrow morning? We could meet for breakfast and I could make some notes.'

She nodded. 'That sounds good to me.'

***

By the time Lucy arrived at her grandmother's cabin it was almost midnight. She had dined with Sheldon and the time had flown by. He was such interesting company and she was looking forward to seeing him again first thing in the morning for his interview, but first she needed to relieve Hetty of her duty to watch her grandmother and stay in the cabin herself. As she entered in the dark, she heard her grandmother's shallow breaths and drew back the curtain to see much to her horror that Hetty was not there at all. Had the girl let her down? But no, surely not if she was as keen as Lucy was to keep watch over the woman and it was Hetty who had told her the nurse was visiting her grandmother's bedroom late at night back home.

Quietly, she left the cabin and rapped urgently on Hetty's cabin door. The door opened quickly as if Hetty had been expecting her. 'Come in quick, Miss, in case she hears us! The nurse has gone for her nightly walk on deck,' she whispered.

Lucy did as told. 'What happened?'

'Well, I was there like you told me to be, hiding in that curtained off area, and all was going well, when about half an hour ago, I heard the door opening and Nurse Carmichael's voice. Oh Miss, she actually woke your grandmother up to give her that medicine. It was horrible, Lady Fanshaw sounded a bit confused and drowsy, but it seems she took the medicine willingly as like I said, I suspect she's addicted to it.'

'But if it all went to plan, why did you leave my grandmother's room?'

Hetty looked down at her feet. 'I'm sorry. I started to hiccup and couldn't stop meself, Miss…' She glanced up at Lucy as if ashamed. 'Then Nurse Carmichael whipped back the curtain and found me.'

'Oh dear,' Lucy said biting on her lip. This had ruined her plans, and now although not Hetty's fault, it had put the woman on her guard. 'What did she say?'

'She was ever so angry and has forbidden me from entering your grandmother's bedroom again at night as she says that only she is to go there from now on.'

'Oh, does she now!' Lucy gritted her teeth and fisted her hands at her side with the anger that was mounting inside of her, but she realised she would need to bide her time.

'But what shall we do now, Miss?'

'For now, we do precisely nothing as to do something would arouse even more suspicion for Nurse Carmichael,' she said firmly, patting Hetty affectionately on her forearm. 'But when we arrive at New York we are going to give that nurse the slip and get a second opinion on my grandmother's condition.'

Hetty beamed. 'I like that sound of that!'

'But just one thing, Hetty…'

'Yes?'

'Whatever you do, do not mention this to anyone on board this ship apart from Sheldon as if that woman gets wind of it, she might cause problems for us.'

'You have my word on that, Miss.' Hetty said winking at her, and as if realising she shouldn't have done so, her hands flew to her face and she muttered, 'Sorry, Miss.'

Lucy laughed. 'No problem, Hetty,' she replied, winking back at the girl.

Chapter Eight

1885

"A Blow to the Head"

'Who on earth is he, Martha?'

Whose hushed female voice was that? Archie groaned as he fought to bring his eyes into focus as a couple of sets of curious eyes peered down at him.

'Look, he's coming around, Nora…' the one called Martha said.

He let out a long sigh and rubbed his head. 'Where am I?' he groaned.

'Yer at The Jolly Roger, an inn, sir,' Nora, who appeared to be the younger of the two said. 'We found you outside, you'd fallen from your 'orse and we brought you in here to rest in one of the bedrooms. But don't worry none about your 'orse—we got one of the ostlers to feed and stable him for the night.'

'You mean I've been lying here all this time, over night?' He pulled himself up on his haunches, squinted and then blinked several times as the sun filtered strongly through the window.

Martha, noticing his discomfort, drew the curtains a little to keep the sun out of his eyes. 'Yes,' she said. 'You've been here since about yesterday noon.'

'All that time!' he said. He had the feeling he should have been somewhere else by now, but where? 'The trouble is, I can't remember much. Where exactly is this?'

'You're about a mile from the docks, sir,' Nora said. 'Looks like you were on your way there. You mumbled something 'bout it before you passed out, but you did take a fair blow to the head.'

He touched his head and felt some sort of bandage in place. 'The docks?'

'Yes.' Nora looked at him. 'We bandaged your head because it was bleeding, though the cut don't look that deep to me, you were lucky as you just missed the cobblestones and hit your head on the dirt track beside them. Must have been one of those little sharp stones what did the damage.'

'Have you no idea why you were headed towards the docks, then?' Martha said with a look of concern on her face.

'No, none whatsoever I'm afraid.'

She shook her head. 'Well maybe it will come back to you later. Let's get you seated in a chair and Nora will fetch you something to eat and a mug of tea.'

He nodded gratefully. 'Thank you.' He patted the top pocket of his waist coat to retrieve his wallet so he could pay them for their time and attention and of course the food, but felt a sickening feeling in the pit of his stomach when he realised it was no longer where it usually was.

'What's the matter, sir?' Martha asked.

'It's my wallet, I can't seem to find it.'

'Don't worry about it,' Martha reassured. 'We put it somewhere safe for you, I'll fetch it for you now as there are people with nifty fingers in this place,' she said knowingly.

He shot her a smile of relief. 'Thank you both so much.'

'Nora, go and fetch the gentleman a bite to eat. What's your name, sir?' Martha asked.

'Archie, Archie Ledbetter.'

'And where do you live, Mr Ledbetter?'

'I think it's somewhere in Whitechapel. No sorry, with my Uncle Walter I think in his big house.' Try as he might, he couldn't remember much, things were hazy for him.

'You take your time, Mr Ledbetter. It might come back to you soon.' Martha turned to glare at Nora. 'Don't stand there gawping, girl! Go and get the gentleman some of that stew and a hunk of bread and a nice mug of sweet tea.'

The girl nodded before scuttling out of the room.

'Nice young lass but a bit slow on the uptake,' Martha explained.

He nodded. His head was throbbing now. 'I wonder why I was headed for the docks?' he asked himself as much as Martha.

'Might you have been going to see someone off somewhere, do you think?'

'Maybe? But I don't know who. Unless it was my Uncle Walter, maybe.' All sorts of memories flooded his mind: his mother's smiling face before him. He remembered how loving she had been and how upset he was when she'd passed away. Ginny, his next-door neighbour and her benevolence towards him, Bessie in Whitechapel and her infamous pies and little Lucy the kitchen maid at the coaching inn.

Lucy!

That's who he had been in a rush to see. But where was she going to? And why?

'I think things are coming back to me but they're not making any sense,' he said, shaking his head.

Martha laid a hand on his shoulder. 'Take your time, sir. There's no rush. Have something to eat and some more rest. I'll fetch a doctor to you. Do you have any money to pay for one?'

He shrugged his shoulders. 'Normally, I might have. I need to check my wallet.'

'I'll just go and fetch it from my secret hiding place. Safe as houses there it is,' she said kindly.

Archie stared outside the leaded window down onto the court yard below. This was some sort of coaching inn by the look of it and the low wooden beams of the bedroom gave the place a Tudor like feel. The room was sparse but clean and basic nevertheless with a large wooden wardrobe, matching chest of drawers and a table with a porcelain bowl and jug atop of it.

Martha returned within a couple of minutes and handed him his leather wallet. 'I've not looked inside,' she said, 'but it feels as if there is something inside of it.'

He took it from her grasp. 'Thank you for being so honest,' he swallowed. Then he opened the wallet to see several sovereigns. 'Yes, I have enough to pay for my board and lodgings here and pay a doctor too.' He handed her a couple of sovereigns. 'For yourself and the lass for helping me,' he said.

She waved her hand in front of his face. 'There's no need. I would do it for anyone.'

'Thank you,' he said, 'but take it, please. You have helped me enormously. I don't know what I'd have done without you.'

She nodded and took the coins and dropped them into her apron pocket. 'I'll be sure to see that Nora gets her share. Make no bones about that!' Seeing the sadness on his face, she added, 'Take a seat at the table and the girl will be along shortly. Is there anything else I can get for you?'

'I'm all right for now. What's your name, Martha what?'

'Martha Timkins,' she replied. 'I'm the landlady here. And don't worry, sir, you can stay with us as long as you need to. I'll just go and hurry that girl along.'

She turned on her heel and left the room leaving him to his thoughts. It was no use, things weren't coming back to him fast enough for his liking. He shook his head and groaned, then turned as he heard the door open and saw Nora arrive carrying a wooden tray. She placed a steaming bowl of stew in front of him with a hunk of bread. 'It's lamb stew, sir,' she said. 'Eat up and I'll bring you a pot of tea now to go with it.'

'Thank you, Nora,' he smiled and began to attack the stew with gusto, taking large mouthfuls. It looked and tasted delicious and the aroma of meat and onions filled the room. He began to slow down as he realised maybe it wouldn't do him any good to eat so quickly. He was ravenous though and soon Nora returned with the tray now containing a pot of tea in a brown earthenware tea pot along with a large mug and plate of what appeared to be some sort of pie with custard. 'It's apple pie, sir,' she said, placing the bowl before him.

He nodded and thanked her and watched her leave. Bless her, even if she was a bit slow as the landlady had described her, she appeared to have a heart of gold.

After eating his fill, the landlady took him downstairs to the stables outside to check on his horse. The horse looked at him as if to ask, 'Where have you been all this time?' Archie stroked him and whispered, 'Atticus…'

'So, you remember his name then?' Martha smiled.

'Yes, I do. It's all coming back to me. I don't live with my uncle any more, I have my own house which I've just inherited from my father. My surname has been changed too—it's no longer Ledbetter like I told you, it's now Pomfrey. I recall it now…I was in my carriage and something happened to the wheel. The coachman and I decided to look for somewhere to stay while it got repaired, we went bareback on the horses but I decided to ride off on my own to try to catch…'

'Who?'

'Lucy, the name I mentioned earlier.' He looked up at the sky for a moment where storm clouds appeared to be gathering overhead as the earlier sunshine abated. 'I remember it now…'

'You do?'

'She was leaving for The Continent with her grandmother who is ill and I'd promised to wave her off. We won't be seeing one another for some months…' Then as if it was right now he realised that he'd missed his only opportunity, he felt his eyes well with tears.

'Well, there's no use me pointing this out to you but you'll not catch her now and you've missed your chance.' She patted his shoulder, affectionately, as if she understood all too well what the girl meant to him. 'So, I reckon you need to stay here at least another day to get your head straight and maybe we'll get the doctor out to you.'

He nodded with a heart full of regret.

Chapter Nine

1874

"A Thief in their Midst"

Archie felt a large hand slap his head, which caused him to recoil backwards against the tiled wall. Turning, expecting to see one of the teachers before him, he realised it was Ashcroft. 'Watch where you're going, you clumsy oaf!' The boy glared at him.

Archie looked up at him and glared back. It was Bill Brackley before him again but there was no use retaliating as there would be no one to save him here, the other boys were too scared to go against the big bully and the teachers would probably back him up as he was a prefect. 'Sorry, Ashcroft,' Archie apologised, though he didn't think he had got in the boy's way but for now he needed to keep the peace to keep himself safe.

'Say that again?' Ashcroft shouted.

'Sorry!'

'You didn't say that the first time, you little tyke, you swore at me!'

'No, I didn't, honest…what I said was, "Sorry, Ashcroft."'

Ashcroft grabbed Archie by the collar of his jacket and shook him. 'It's *sir* to you and don't you forget it!'

Archie trembled. 'S…sorry, sir.'

Ashcroft pushed him roughly so that Archie hurt his shoulder against the wall. 'Ow!' he grimaced, then he rubbed it. That was painful. He watched as the older lad made off down the corridor, probably in search of someone else to bully. He huffed out a breath, he needed to do something to put a stop to all of this, but what?

***

The answer came in the form of something advertised on the notice board at the gymnasium.

Ever considered boxing lessons?

A meeting will be held here at the gym on Friday evening at 6 o'clock sharp.

Most of the lads in his dorm weren't interested in after school activities unless there was something in it for them, but Archie said nothing about his thoughts about boxing but on Friday night made his way to the gym.

When he arrived, there were only three other boys there from other dormitories, none he had ever been introduced to and all looked bigger and older than he was but they were friendly towards him, unlike most of the boys in his dorm. By the time he'd had his first lesson which consisted of learning how to defend himself using his fists and fast footwork, he knew he'd made the right decision because in a few weeks' time, no one would ever dare bully him again.

***

'You're looking pleased with yourself!' Carruthers stared at him waiting for an answer as Wally plonked himself down on Archie's bed, munching on some sort of pie.

''ere, where'd you get that from?' Archie asked without bothering to reply to Carruthers.

Wally swallowed a morsel before replying, 'Matron. She's doling out some of the food from the hampers as Old Penny has told her we worked hard this week…'

Archie and Carruthers dashed off leaving Wally to his pie. 'I can't wait to get my hands on my hamper!' Carruthers shouted as he flew down the corridor.

Archie couldn't either as he knew Cook had baked his favourites for him but was disappointed to see the size of the queue before him. He kicked his foot against the wall. He'd been waiting all week for this and now he had to wait even longer.

'You still haven't answered me, why were you looking so pleased earlier?'

Archie drew close to his friend and whispered, 'I've started to take boxing lessons!'

'Boxing lessons?' Carruthers blurted out.

'Sssh, I don't want the others to know. No one else from our class is doing it, I'm in a group with some older lads. I really enjoyed it.'

Carruthers looked on with admiration in his eyes. 'Can I come along to the next class?'

'You can if you like but this is something I really want to do.'

'I'll come and watch then and see if I like it.'

'All right,' replied Archie as the queue surged forward.

It was ten minutes before they got to see Matron. 'Archibald Pomfrey,' she said studying the book in her hand. To Archie she sounded as if she had a plum in her mouth with her overly refined accent. He'd met her sort before in Whitechapel. He'd once heard Cook at Huntington Hall refer to that sort as "all blethering bumptiousness and no bloomers!" And in Matron's case, he guessed she was right.

He nodded.

'Well are you or aren't you he?'

'Yes, Matron Bagley. I am that boy.'

She glared at him. He was well aware that she already knew his name so why was she making a big song and dance about it?

She waggled a piece of paper before his eyes. 'According to my list, in your hamper you have various cakes and pieces of fruit and two rounds of cheese. You are allowed one piece of fruit and one cake to take away with you. Come along inside and choose.'

He entered the room with trepidation as he didn't much trust the old crone as he knew for a fact sometimes, she summoned certain pupils to give them a leathering for various misdemeanours.

He glanced around. Piles of wicker hampers were neatly stacked with each boy's name tag attached with a piece of string. Matron located Archie's hamper. She knelt down to open it up, displaying various cakes covered in pieces of muslin cloth which she unwrapped before him. 'There appears to be a chocolate cake, a plain sponge and a fruit cake. Which one would you like?'

His mouth watered at the thought of such delights. 'I think I'll have the chocolate one, please!' he said with great excitement.

She looked up at him over her spectacles. 'On second thoughts, I think you need to pick between the other two.'

Archie's heart sank, he was so disappointed. He waited a moment as if he thought she might have a change of heart, but by the look in her eyes he soon realised she would not be swayed on the subject.

But why couldn't he have his favourite chocolate cake right now? It just wasn't fair.

'I'll have the plain sponge one then please, Mrs Bagley,' he said, with his head lowered. All his earlier enthusiasm had ebbed away. He liked Cook's plain sponge cake but he'd really set his mind on her rich chocolate cake with its cocoa buttercream and chocolate icing.

Matron stood and huffing, she handed him the cake, which felt smaller than he was expecting, but he said nothing. He waited whilst Carruthers went through the same rigmarole. He ended up coming away with a hunk of cheese and an apple, he didn't have such a sweet tooth as Archie.

When they returned to the dorm, Wally was still on the bed brushing the crumbs of evidence of his pork pie away from his mouth with his fingertips.

He sat forward when he saw the boys, his eyes enlarging in anticipation. 'Well, what did you both get?' he asked.

'Cheese and an apple!' Carruthers said.

'Didn't you get anything more interesting than that?' Wally scoffed.

'Well, I like them!'

Wally turned his attention to Archie. 'What about you?'

'A sponge cake,' Archie muttered without much enthusiasm.

'What's the matter?' Wally eyed him up as if he were speaking in a foreign tongue.

Archie shrugged. 'Nothing really.'

'He's blooming disappointed as he wanted his chocolate cake and he got just a plain sponge cake,' Carruthers supplied. 'Look, what's the matter? At least you've got a bleeding cake!'

Archie laid the muslin wrapped cake on the bed. 'Look at this!' he exclaimed, 'I thought it felt small. Someone has cut off half of this cake!'

The boys stared as Archie opened the cloth to reveal an unevenly cut sponge cake.

'Surely not!' Wally seemed as outraged as Archie was. 'Why would they do that and how do you know?'

'I've no idea,' Archie shook his head sadly. 'But I intend to find out.'

'But how?' Carruthers blinked several times.

'I'm going to ask all the other boys if any of their stuff has gone missing or been cut in half like that!'

***

Following further investigation, it came to light that several boys in the dorm had items missing from their hampers too, or cakes and hunks of cheese cut in half.

'But how are we going to find out if Matron is stealing from us?' A boy called Wilmslow asked.

'I don't think it's Matron taking our food,' Archie said firmly, 'it's more than her position here is worth. I'm going to stop up tonight and watch her store room, but I'm going to need you boys to take it in turns to keep watch. Maybe she sometimes forgets to lock the door and that's when the thief or thieves must be slipping in.'

The boys nodded in agreement, and it was the first time ever that Archie held their confidence and it felt good that they were fighting for a common cause. It wouldn't be too much bother for him to stay up late and keep watch as he'd been used to being out late with Bill Brackley, who had trawled him and Bobby around various pubs in the Whitechapel area following a day of chimney sweeping at all those fancy houses with rich pickings.

It was arranged that Carruthers, Wilmslow and Wally would take it in turns to stay on watch duty to warn Archie if they saw Matron or one of the teachers coming anywhere near, whilst Archie hid himself in Matron's store room. Luckily, she'd forgotten to lock the door once again, so slipping inside was easy.

It was a couple of hours after lights out as Archie hid beneath the wooden counter with a blanket over him that he heard a sudden noise. He'd left his pillows behind so that Wally could arrange them in his bed to make it appear as if he lay slumbering when Matron carried out her regular rounds. He hoped he'd get away with it as usually she checked twice during the night with a flickering candle and didn't tend to check up close to the beds. A couple of the boys would disturb the dorm during the night as they needed the lavatory which was permissible as long as they didn't make too much a habit of it.

He held his breath as something furry ran over his hand and he realised it was a rat. It didn't scare him too much as he was used to the rats that ran amok in the East End, though he realised it would freak out most of the other lads who were shielded from such unpleasantries.

He must have dosed off as later he woke with a start to hear the door creak open and a voice say excitedly, 'Come on, Moore! Speed up, why don't you?' The familiar voice hissed.

Ashcroft and Samuel Moore!

'I don't want to do this, we might get caught,' he heard Samuel say. There was real fear in his voice.

'Don't be a sissy. Now I want that chocolate cake from Pomfrey's hamper and some bread and cheese from one of the others, and I spotted a nice large pork pie in one of them as well.' He chuckled. 'We can feast ourselves throughout the night.'

Then he heard another set of footsteps approach and Ashcroft whispered, 'Sssh, hide somewhere.'

There was a scuffle as Ashworth scrambled beneath a wooden counter and to Archie's horror, Samuel clambered under the opposite counter he was hiding under. Both boys stared at one another as Samuel held the flickering candle in his hand. Archie put his finger to his lips to warn him. Samuel said nothing but seemed relieved that Archie allowed him to hide there with him.

He suddenly blew the candle out as the footsteps got closer and they heard a woman's voice shout out, 'Who's in here? Make yourself known or I shall fetch the headmaster!'

Oh no, Matron Bagley!

Archie trembled from top to toe and he felt Samuel do the same beside him.

'Got you!' He heard her yell. 'Now what are you doing in here?'

'I thought I saw one of the younger lads go in here' Ashcroft was saying.

'A likely tale. I've noticed that whenever I come in here lately it looks as if someone has disturbed things.'

'It wasn't me, Mrs Bagley, honest, it wasn't,' Ashcroft said with some conviction.

Matron harrumphed as if giving him the benefit of the doubt.

'Return to your bed, boy! If I see you here once more then I shall have to report you. On second thoughts, I'll escort you to your dorm myself and then I'm coming back here to lock this door!'

There was the sound of departing footsteps as both retreated and then a sigh of relief by Samuel as the door clicked shut behind them. 'Thanks for not telling on me,' he said to Archie. 'But what are you doing in here yourself?'

'I was lying in wait to see who has been pinching food from the other boys' hampers.'

'Well now you know,' Samuel said. 'I never wanted to be a part of this but Ashcroft is heavy with his fists if you understand me?'

Archie nodded, understanding all too well and felt a sudden pang of empathy for the lad. 'I do indeed as I've had a taste of it from him myself. So how long has he been doing this for?'

'Since the start of term but now he's getting greedy and making it obvious. He keeps most of the food for himself anyhow.'

'You'd better get back to bed in case Matron notices you're missing as I bet Ashcroft won't stick up for you if she finds out you're not in your bed. She said she's coming back to lock the door, so we'd better get out of here sharpish!'

'You're right,' Samuel said. 'There's only one person Ashcroft looks out for and that's himself.' He rose to his feet. 'Now you know, you'd better get back to your dorm yourself.'

They were now plunged into darkness and would have to find their way out. 'Can you light your candle?' Archie asked hopefully.

'We better not, in case we're spotted,' the boy replied. 'How did you know where to go in the dark anyhow?'

'There was a light shining through the landing window from the moon, but when I got in here it was pitch black, but I knew where the counter was and that I could hide beneath it as Matron took me behind there once to look in my hamper.'

'We best get out under the cover of darkness to be on the safe side. At least your dorm is nearby, I've got a fair way to go yet.'

Archie did sympathise with the lad and realised he was speaking sense. Once they managed to make their way tentatively to the door, there was ample moonlight in the corridor for Archie to return to his dorm, but first he said his goodbyes to Samuel.

'I won't forget this,' the older boy said. 'Thank you.'

'That's all right. If you bump into Matron on your way back tell her you've been to the lavatory.'

'I will, thank you. I can't say I'd have done the same covering for you mind as Ashcroft, if he'd found out, would lynch me but in this case I felt we were on equal footing.'

'You're right and as he was nabbed by Matron first, there's no need for him to know I'm on to him, is there?'

'No indeed,' said Samuel, patting his new found friend on the shoulder before quietly departing for his own dorm.

Archie heaving a sigh of relief, made it back to his bed, where Wally was pleased to see him and apologised profusely for failing to stay awake long enough to warn him that Matron was on the way. The boy wanted to know what had happened but Archie whispered he'd explain everything in the morning and he promptly fell into a deep slumber almost as soon as his head hit the pillow.

Chapter Ten

1885

"Lady Liberty"

The ship entered New York Bay sounding out its hooter and pumping out steam as Lucy gasped with delight to finally arrive in America. She stood with others on the ship's deck as they took in the sweep of the bay with all its many buildings in the background and the Statue known as "Liberty Enlightening the World" in the foreground. She felt an arm drape around her shoulder. Turning, she saw Sheldon stood beside her with a big beaming smile on his face. 'Home for me at last!' he exclaimed excitedly. 'Gee, it sure feels like I've been gone a long time!'

She couldn't help being swept along by his enthusiasm. 'This is like something I've never seen before. I mean we have big statues in our country to represent various things but I can't say I've seen anything as big or dramatic as that Lady Liberty statue before!'

Sheldon nodded. 'It took quite a feat of engineering for that to be assembled. It's a neoclassical sculpture of the highest order!' he announced, brimming with pride.

'Yes, it is.' Lucy marvelled at how it stood out welcoming people to the shores of America.

'It's the first structure folk see when they land here. All those people arriving from so many countries. Do you know, New York is such a multi-cultural place? People arrive here from Great Britain, Ireland, Italy, Spain, Eastern Europe, Scandinavia…I could go on and on. And Lucy, you shall see what I mean when you visit all the different retail outlets and eating establishments. It's such a vibrant, growing city. A metropolis of modernity!'

Lucy frowned, feeling that somehow Sheldon must think she was old fashioned and behind the times. 'I suppose my country must seem a tad backward to you?'

'Oh, no, no, no!' He chuckled as he wagged his index finger in her face. 'I enjoyed my last visit very much, though I think your class system is different to over here. Here, anyone can do anything, but in your country, there is a big class divide between the "haves" and the "have nots". I saw that for myself first hand when I mingled with the people of Whitechapel. There are many hardships. I'm not saying we don't have those kinds of things here, because it does happen, but not to the extent it does in London.'

Lucy contemplated it was sad that people could live near to one another where one might be struggling to survive to find food and shelter and within a couple of miles, someone else might be living in a large house where money was no object and there was much extravagance and decadence going on. Waste even. She'd witnessed both in her short life. Whitechapel was a seedy, crime-ridden area where people lived in abject poverty. She cast her mind back to its sweatshops, dosshouses, sprawling slums, factories, warehouses and abattoirs. The pubs and the coaching inn she had once worked at attracted all manner of society from the city gent to the lowly char lady. Disease and malnutrition of its folk was so widespread that some would die before the end of childhood.

It seemed to her that there were three class divisions not just the "haves" and the "have nots". There were those that were poor but they had jobs working as labourers, shopkeepers or tailors. Then there was the very poor who were often women with a houseful of children who might get casual work as seamstresses to supplement their husbands' meagre earnings or lack thereof, or else they slogged it out at wash houses. And then there were the homeless who tried but often failed to get a night's lodging and a day's food to fill their bellies. They were the hardest to see on the streets. And to think that Sheldon had lived amongst them all to highlight the issue. But why? What was in it for him? She wondered.

She swallowed. 'What made you decide to live amongst the people of the East End of London?' she blurted out to her horror, as she hadn't much thought about what she'd been about to say and hadn't wished to offend him.

He cleared his throat and looked deep into her eyes, as he explained, 'Someone in New York referred to the area of London's Whitechapel as being "An Urban Jungle". He had just returned from there himself and spoke of "slum dwellers". So fascinated was I that I wanted to see it for myself. I used to work as a reporter on the New York Tribune, and initially, I wrote articles about it and dispatched them to my editor for publication. In time, I had amassed a lot of information. The newspaper received lots of positive communication about the articles and it was suggested that I write a book. So, I stayed on longer than intended and even employed the work of a local artist so I can include various impressions of the people and the area in the book.'

'Do you think I might see the sketches at some time?' she angled her head to look up at him.

'For sure. When we reach New York, I shall show you my portfolio of work. The experiences related to me from the people I met in London's underworld turned me into somewhat of an explorer. I wanted to see the evidence with my own eyes not just what my acquaintance had told me. It was far worse than anything he had ever told me about. I was living right in the heart of it, rubbing shoulders with thieves, prostitutes, gamblers, beggars and more. But he, that gentleman, only saw things at arms' length. I witnessed for myself the abject poverty and degradation which was far more serious than anything I ever witnessed in my homeland...' he said sadly, shaking his head. He held on to the ship's rail as if trying to compose himself after thinking about his time in Whitechapel.

Lucy touched his arm. 'It's good work that you've been doing,' she said kindly, intending to lift his spirits, 'and to be applauded, not everyone could do what you've just done,' she said with great admiration.

'The East End is like a bottomless pit. "Invoke not the unhallowed spirits of the abyss; invoke the spotless synod of the Gods..."'

'Pardon?' She quirked a brow at him.

'It's a quote by English novelist and philosopher, William Godwin.' He smiled. 'I think of it every time I think of Whitechapel.'

Lucy wasn't too sure she completely understood, as he appeared to her to be a well-educated, highly literate gentleman. *Why on earth does he want to be in my company? I was just a kitchen maid until my grandmother took me in and I discovered I had been born in the world of "haves" instead of the "have nots".*

'For London the East End slums are an immeasurably deep abyss, where the people are doomed to a life of degradation, misery and suffering,' he said solemnly. 'The urban jungle, as my friend dubbed it, has caused a sub human culture of a class warfare and appalling conditions.'

She couldn't argue with that and said no more as they both stood staring at the statue before them as it enlarged as they got closer and closer to the bay.

***

After their documentation was checked on landing, they all took a carriage to Sheldon's house. Lucy gasped as she took in all the various buildings along the way. Even the people looked so vibrant and fashionable here: ladies strolling along with their frilled parasols to keep the sun off their faces in their bustle-style dresses, gentlemen in well-tailored suits and straw boaters. Even Nurse Carmichael looked enamoured with the place. After travelling for some time where they all spoke excitedly to one another as Grandma slept for most of the journey, the carriage swept up a long drive way until it came to a shuddering halt. Sheldon's house was like no other that Lucy had ever seen before. The red brick mansion stood loud and proud, dominating the surrounding landscape. Its turreted towers looming and large above the arched airy windows.

'Sheldon, your house is wonderful. It has such character!' Lucy gasped, clasping both hands together as she gazed at it in awe as they both stood outside the property.

'It's set in an acre and a half of land,' he said proudly. 'It's three storeys high, has five bathrooms, ten bedrooms, four marble fire places and a two-storey carriage house in the grounds,' he said with a smile. 'But alas, it is not mine, well not at the moment, it belonged to my father. He had this house built at the beginning of the Civil War.'

Lucy wondered why he said "belonged". Maybe his father no longer lived here or else had passed away? It might be churlish to ask him right now when he had just arrived back home, in the country of his birth, and what a beautiful, vibrant area this was and all. It fair near robbed her of her breath.

Nurse Carmichael, Hetty and Grandma were still seated in the open top carriage that Sheldon had hired to bring them all to his home. Grandma had a plaid blanket draped over her knees to keep her warm and they were chatting in an animated fashion, but Lucy couldn't hear what was being discussed even though she could tell by the nodding of heads and smiles that they were as much in awe of the property as herself.

Sheldon turned back towards the trio and shouted, 'If you ladies will give us both a moment, I shall send my staff out to attend to you all.' He slipped the carriage driver some coinage and the man tipped his hat as a sign of respect.

Grandma smiled and shooed Sheldon away with her white gloved hand as if to indicate that was fine with her. Lucy could tell how much her grandmother liked Sheldon especially as he had insisted, she stay as a guest at the family home.

As Lucy followed him into the house, she gasped at the hand-crafted walnut curved staircase in the hallway. This house was just as fine as her grandmother's but in a different way. Whereas Grandma's was full of splendour with expensive and lavish furnishings, this one was vibrant and modern looking.

A middle-aged lady in long mauve dress with lace edged collar and cuffs came charging towards them. 'Sheldon, darling,' she opened both her arms ready to embrace him. Lucy was surprised that she had an English accent. He hugged the woman for a moment, which was a display of affection she wasn't used to at her grandmother's home where things were very formal indeed. Then Lucy realised this lady must be Sheldon's mother.

The woman stepped away and with twinkling china blue eyes she studied Lucy, her eyes crinkling at the sides as she smiled broadly at her. She had such a nice honest face that Lucy couldn't help immediately warming towards her.

'And this, Mother,' Sheldon introduced, 'is Miss Lucy Fanshaw.'

'Enchanted to meet you, dear,' she said holding out her long, elegant hand for Lucy to take.

'Thank you for welcoming us into your home.' Lucy smiled and shook the woman's hand.

'It's a pleasure, my dear. I asked Mrs Marten, our housekeeper, to prepare your rooms when Sheldon wired me to say you were all on your way. But I'm being rude as you've had such a long journey, I'll ask Cook to prepare a little something for you all.'

Sheldon laid his hand on his mother's shoulder. 'Thank you, Mother.' Lucy could see the deep affection they had for one another.

Shortly, they were all seated around a table that was laid with a pretty white lace tablecloth and colourful floral china nicely set out. The room overlooked what appeared to be some sort of orchard and as the sun filtered through the large arch window, Lucy gazed at Sheldon as he spoke animatedly to everyone. Grandma and Hetty hung on to his every word. It was at that moment Lucy fell deeply in love with him.

Chapter Eleven

1874

"Accepted at Last"

Before they were called from their dorm to breakfast in the hall, the boys gathered around Archie to find out what they could about the previous night. There was a lot of chatter and hustle and bustle in the excitement of it all. Some were jostling forward, nudging with their elbows to get near him or pushing others in exasperation for them to get out of the way.

When he noticed what was happening, Archie tutted under his breath and holding up his vertical palm said, 'Please can you give everyone some breathing space, boys?'

The bustle died down as they waited in awe to hear what he had to say. If someone had dropped a pin as they awaited with baited breath, it would have been heard by one and all. 'I've discovered who the perpetrator is!' Archie said with great conviction. 'Matron caught him in the act last night!'

The boys drew nearer. 'Who was it then?' One of them shouted.

'Ashcroft. He's been doing it for weeks, apparently without anyone suspecting him,' said Archie smugly as he folded his arms and smiled with a look on his face that said, 'Forewarned is forearmed.'

Wilfred, who was taller than the other boys, stared hard in his direction. 'How could you possibly know that?' he questioned.

'I, er, heard Matron say so,' he replied, which wasn't the complete truth as it was Samuel Moore who had informed him of this but he didn't want to get the lad into trouble.

Wilfred nodded. 'Well at least it won't be happening any more now Matron Bagley's in the picture.'

The other boys murmured in agreement. There was no chance for them to discuss it further as the bell clanged at the end of the corridor to summon them to prayers and then breakfast.

***

Throughout breakfast, Archie tried to avoid Samuel's gaze not to put the boys onto him but at one-point Samuel smiled at him, and as the boys were busy tucking in to their bacon and fried eggs, Archie returned his smile.

The past few weeks Archie felt he had grown a little as the cuffs on his shirts and jackets were now barely fitting him. His fitness level had also improved due to the boxing lessons he was participating in, and he had taken to other exercise too such as running around the lake and use of a skipping rope, one hundred rotations morning and night. At first, he barely managed the half mile around the lake, but soon he was managing several rounds a day. None of the other boys in his dorm were that interested in sport apart from rugby, they all seemed to want to play that but weren't allowed to in the first year. Yet, Archie wondered how they could possibly want to participate if they weren't fit enough in the first place for it.

It was almost the end of the day when one of the six formers entered the classroom to speak to Old Penny. Wally and Carruthers grinned as whenever someone entered, the master became distracted chatting away to their unexpected visitor who often turned out to be another teacher or senior pupil at the school. During the distraction, the boys had time to mess about and even got away with throwing ink pellet papers at one another at times. But on this occasion, Mr Pennyworth immediately addressed the class.

His gaze was drawn to Archie as he felt his stomach somersault. 'Archibald Pomfrey,' he said in a solemn tone, 'the headmaster would like to see you in his office, immediately,' Penny stressed.

'Archie's for the cane! Archie's for the cane!' Wilfred shouted, egged on by the other boys. Only Wally and Carruthers remained silent as they sat there open mouthed.

'Pipe down!' the master shouted as he slapped his willow cane down hard onto the desk before him, causing the boys to look at one another in fear. Mild mannered Old Penny was angry with them which was most unusual. 'Archie is most certainly not for the cane, but one of you lot might be if you carry on shouting!'

A deathly hush took over the classroom after the six former had departed with Archie in tow. Then Mr Pennyworth said in a quieter tone, 'Open your text books to page twenty-one, read the lesson and then complete the exercise. You have twenty minutes each. Then leave your exercise books on my desk for marking. And I don't want to hear a pip out of any of you!'

As Archie marched along the corridor in the direction of the headmaster's office, the six former suddenly turned towards him and said, 'I know what you did!'

Archie shuddered as he feared a beating, but then the lad smiled at him. 'You were very brave to hide in Matron's room. Ashcroft is going to have his comeuppance some day!'

'How'd you know what I did?' Archie asked. Had Samuel let him down with their secret, he wondered?

'One of the lads in my dorm saw you and Samuel in the corridor, he was on watch. Don't worry, he's only told me about it—that's all and I'm completely on your side.'

Archie felt a satisfaction in knowing this and not only now did the other boys in his dorm seem to have accepted him, at least two older lads had too. Maybe Ashcroft wasn't all that well liked then? Maybe his peers at the school only seemed to favour him because they really feared him and maybe, just maybe, this would prove to be his Achilles heel.

***

Archie rapped on the headmaster's door tentatively and the six-form boy left him there, no doubt to return to his studies. 'Good luck, Archie,' he said before departing.

Archie nodded nervously, concerned as to just what awaited him.

'Enter!' Boomed a strong voice from within.

Slowly, Archie turned the brass knob, his palms soaked with perspiration.

'Ah, Pomfrey,' the headmaster said. 'Close the door behind you, boy.'

Archie did as instructed, standing with his hands behind his back to face the man, as the boys were told to do in front of their elders at the school.

Mr Criddlington twirled his long grey moustache for a moment as if thinking carefully of what he was to say next. Was the man about to whip out his cane which was kept in the cupboard in the corner of the room? Had he found out about last night's caper? Was that why Samuel Moore had been smiling at him during breakfast as he was intending on telling on him? Or had Ashcroft got there first? But surely Samuel at least wouldn't dob him in as else he'd be in trouble himself for being in Matron's room in the first place with all those hampers containing goodies from home.

Archie's eyes diverted right and he was relieved to see the long cupboard door was locked, but what if he'd hidden the cane under his desk? In Archie's mind he imagined that somehow word had got back to the man in one form or another that he was out of his bed and hiding in Matron's room that night.

Mr Criddlington looked at Archie with a great deal of sympathy in his eyes. He cleared his throat. 'There's no easy way to say this so I'll just come out and say it to you...'

Archie's knees buckled beneath him and he fought to stay upright. Noticing this, the headmaster added, 'Please take a seat young man, I'm sure it will be easier for you.'

Archie nodded and took the seat opposite the desk from the man. It was practically unheard of for any pupil to take a seat in the headmaster's room. 'I'm afraid it's not good news...your uncle has sustained an accident. You're needed back home.'

'Uncle Walter?' Archie's lips trembled as tears sprang to his eyes, though of course that was a silly question as he had no other uncle but just by saying the words, he had to know for sure.

The headmaster nodded then steepled his fingers on the desk in front of him. 'There's some sort of concussion involved too. Apparently, he slipped on some wet rocks when he was out fishing and sustained a head injury.'

Oh no, this couldn't be happening again! That's what had happened to his half-brother and he'd died because of it, but his head injury was due to a fall from his horse.

'W…when did this happen, Sir?'

'Yesterday afternoon,' Mr Criddlington said grimly, as he shook his head then rubbed his chin as if deliberating carefully what he was to say next. 'The staff from the house have sent for you. I think it was the cook who has asked for you to return home, just in case.'

Just in case of what?

'Thank you, Sir,' Archie said trying to hold back great big gulping sobs that were threatening to engulf him.

The headmaster stood and, drawing near to Archie's side, laid a hand on his shoulder. 'Be brave, Archie. You shall be given compassionate leave of absence from this school for time being. Go and pack your trunk and my carriage will be waiting for you outside. I'll send a member of staff to accompany you. I'm afraid you need to prepare for the worse, just in case though. Remember, although you are so young, those members of staff will need guidance right now, understood?'

Archie nodded, though he didn't really understand. How was he to know what to do in such circumstances? 'Yes, Sir,' he said meekly.

'Now go back to your dormitory and pack your belongings and someone shall be waiting for you outside.'

***

Archie's head was in such a spin, he didn't know what he was throwing into his trunk all together but it wouldn't really matter as he still had some clothing at his uncle's home. Right now, his choice of clothing was the last thing on his mind. All he cared about was getting back home to see his uncle. It was funny to think at one time he had really feared Uncle Walter until he got to know and love the man, realising that he'd always had his best interests at heart.

Wally and Carruthers entered the dorm. 'We came to see what's going on?' Wally said drawing near.

'It's my uncle,' Archie replied sadly as his eyes misted over. He broke down in tears, the same tears he'd been holding back at the headmaster's office.

He heard Carruthers whisper to Wally. 'The fellow must have died.'

Archie vehemently shook his head. 'No. Not yet anyhow, he's had some sort of blow to his head when he slipped whilst out fishing,' he sniffed. 'I don't know no more than that but the staff have summoned me back to the house.'

'Then we won't hold you up no longer,' Wally said kindly. He patted Archie on the shoulder. 'You've got a big trunk so we'll carry it between us for you.'

Archie was amazed at the kindness of his friends and would have broken down once more, but he had no time for that as now he needed to be on the road. Who knew what would face him when he returned home?

As the boys walked along the dark corridors towards the daylight outside. His friends huffed and puffed as they struggled to carry the heavy trunk, but Archie was unaware of this as he felt as though he were in a dream. This couldn't be happening, could it? Any moment now Matron would enter the dorm and call them to get up. 'Get out of those lazy beds, boys! I want you washed and dressed and ready for inspection before you go for prayers and breakfast. Clean finger nails! No tidemarks on your necks! And no potatoes growing in those ears!' What he wouldn't give to hear her say those words right now.

The trio descended the steps at the entrance to the school, Wally and Carruthers still struggling with the heavy trunk as Archie looked at the lady stood beside the coach. He knew that face but she looked more fanciful than usual in a very becoming brown hat with matching cape, with floral dress beneath. It was the lady from the dining room who served them up their food and often winked at him when no one was watching. He was so glad it was her.

'Hello, Archie. I'm Mrs Brewster. You obviously recognise me from the dining hall?'

He nodded. 'Yes, Ma'am.'

'Well come along as we best be on our way, I've brought some food for the journey as you'll be missing out at lunch time.'

He followed her into the carriage as the trunk was loaded on top by the driver. Wally and Carruthers stood to wave him off and

Archie popped his head out of the coach window. 'Thank you both!' He shouted.

They waved back in silence.

Then Archie settled himself down against the leather upholstery and let out a long breath. Who knew what awaited him at Huntington Hall?

Chapter Twelve

"A Plan is Devised"
1885

After they'd eaten, Sheldon took Lucy to one side. 'Might I speak to you in private for a moment?' he asked.

She nodded.

'Meet me in the drawing room in a few minutes,' he said discretely, 'don't tell anyone. It's the next room down the corridor.'

Nurse Carmichael glared at her, making her feel most uncomfortable. Lucy got the distinct impression that the woman was not pleased that the plans her grandmother had were now disturbed. They were supposed to be booking into a hotel near Manhattan. As far as Lucy was concerned, the woman seemed to wield her power over everyone and if questions were asked, she'd reply, *'It's doctor's orders!' or 'Look, these are medical issues that you know nothing about!'* whilst wagging her index finger beneath their noses. It was all a smokescreen for her arrogant behaviour, Lucy felt. You couldn't tell the woman anything as she insisted she knew what was best.

So, it was with some relief that Sheldon had arranged to speak privately with her. As she entered the drawing room, he came towards her and took her hands in his own. For a moment, it seemed so intimate almost as if he were about to kiss her and her heart was beginning to melt in that moment, but then he stepped away and closed the door in a furtive manner.

'I'm sorry to do things this way but from what you've told me about your grandmother's nurse, I think it's best we are not disturbed?'

Lucy nodded, grateful that he understood the predicament she was in. 'Yes, she seems to oppose everything I suggest.' She smiled in a sardonic fashion, hoping he'd understand her predicament.

His eyes lit up. 'Then how about this? First thing tomorrow morning, we'll get your grandmother out of here and to my physician to be examined? I can send word to him via one of the servants tonight so that he will be prepared.'

'That sounds very good to me,' Lucy replied, feeling full of admiration for the man and how he took charge of things. She chewed her lip for a moment.

'What's the matter? You look concerned.'

'I'm worried about the cost. Grandmother has money to pay of course, but will it be expensive?'

Sheldon shook his head. 'No, not at all. Let me take care of it, Dr Meyer is an eminent physician here. He owes me a little favour anyhow. He can thoroughly examine your grandmother and make his assessment. No charge whatsoever.' He said with a flourish of his hand.

Although this should have placated her, it didn't for some reason and maybe it was because she didn't like to be beholden to anyone. Least of all someone she hadn't known for all that long, no matter how charming he was, nor regarding the feeling of passion she had for him either. But she soon changed her mind when she saw Nurse

Carmichael out in the corridor when she left the room. The woman was ushering her grandmother upstairs to the bedroom.

'Time for your medication and a little nap upstairs…' Nurse Carmichael coaxed.

'Very well, Nurse,' Lady Fanshaw replied in an affable fashion.

Lucy paused a moment. 'Nurse, maybe my grandmother would like to sit out in the garden and enjoy the sunshine, after all, it is such a lovely day and quite warm for this time of the year.'

The nurse glared at her. 'The doctor has put Lady Fanshaw in my care and she's due her evening medication now.'

Lucy decided not to argue with the woman as tomorrow she'd hopefully find out more about her grandmother's condition. 'Very well,' she said curtly. 'You know best.' She didn't want to arouse the woman's suspicions so figured she'd best go along with her plans for time being, and so she went in search of Hetty to check the girl was settling in to the house.

She found Hetty upstairs in the bedroom she'd been allotted. The girl's eyes were as wide as saucers. 'Might I come in?' she asked.

'Oh, you don't have to ask, Miss,' Hetty said as she sat on the bed and smoothed down the counterpane. 'This is luxury itself.'

'I know,' Lucy said as she realised that Hetty only had a bare basic attic room back at home but she was treated as a guest here so had, in theory, gone up in the world.

Lucy shut the door behind her to tell her what was planned for early tomorrow morning and to warn her that whatever she did she was not to let on to the nurse what would happen.

***

Sunlight filtered through the windows of the fancy town house as dawn broke the following morning. Lucy was ready with her grandmother at the back door of the property and as they were about to leave, Hetty showed up with a small bundle wrapped in a muslin cloth. Hugging the bundle close to her chest she said, 'The cook thought to give you this as you won't have had time for breakfast,' she said, looking up at Lucy as the girl held out her hand to pass it on.

'Please thank her for her kindness,' Lucy said taking the bundle from Hetty.

Sheldon appeared at their side. 'I can arrange for a pot of coffee when we arrive at Dr Meyer's consulting room,' he smiled. 'The main thing for now is for us to leave here before a certain someone arises and realises Lady Fanshaw is no longer in her bed…' he said in a surreptitious manner.

Lucy glanced at Hetty. 'When Nurse Carmichael awakes, tell her you were told we'd left to visit someone but don't tell her who. Just be vague about things.'

'Yes, miss.' Hetty bobbed a curtesy and then turned on her heel and entered the back door of the property. Lucy just hoped the girl wouldn't give the game away, but what could she do anyhow? Even if Nurse Carmichael knew where they were headed, there would be nothing she could do to prevent the consultation taking place. But one thing she knew for sure, the woman would be very angry indeed as she saw the sole care of Lady Fanshaw belonging to her and her alone. She was acting on behalf of Grandma's physician when he wasn't around.

Lucy assisted her grandmother into the carriage. The woman's bones were weary with age, but she suspected she was getting used to being in bed so much and not exercising her limbs enough thanks to the nurse and her insistence on keeping Grandma as an invalid. Then Lucy settled herself down beside her grandmother, making sure her legs were covered with the tartan rug provided, as Sheldon sat opposite them.

Sheldon caught Lucy's eyes for a moment and she saw something within them. Almost a devil may care kind of look that she found disturbingly exciting, but this was neither the time nor the place for such frivolity. For time being, her main concern was her grandmother's welfare.

***

About an hour later, having time to finish their repast, the carriage drew up outside a tall redbrick building with an impressive arched doorway and large windows. The sign read: Eastvale Community Hospital. Even at this early hour, several people were milling up and down the steps. Some were nurses in navy serge capes, probably about to begin their duties on the wards. Others were entering the hospital as if wishing to be attended to as patients. Around the side of the building, she noticed a black horse drawn ambulance where two men in uniform and peaked hats, were removing a stretchered case from the back of it.

Sheldon interrupted her thoughts for a moment before explaining, 'This used to be a dispensary styled hospital but then it served as a temporary Civil War tent facility for the returning Union Army wounded men. It's recently had a rebirth as a fully equipped hospital. We have some fine physicians working here and a few new innovative surgical procedures have taken place.'

Lucy nodded, totally in awe. It seemed like such a busy place to her.

They alighted from the carriage and both she and Sheldon helped Lady Fanshaw down from it. 'Do you think you can manage the hospital steps?' Lucy asked her grandmother with some concern. Her legs seemed so weak of late, almost as though she could barely stand unassisted but that would be due to muscle weakness, she supposed.

'Don't you concern yourself about that,' Sheldon said confidently. 'We'll take Lady Fanshaw through the side area where the casualties are assessed.'

Lucy smiled. 'All right, Grandma. You won't have to climb those steps; Mr Brown says we can go in through that entrance over there!'

Her grandmother nodded as if relieved. Lately, Lucy was finding she had to repeat herself to the woman. Was it due to the sort of deafness that came on sometimes with old age? Or was it due to the medication that nurse was plying her with, she wondered?

They walked slowly at Grandma's pace to the casualty unit as they supported her by taking her by the arm, one either side. Drawing near, Lucy was surprised by the loud commotion coming from within. As they entered the unit, she noticed the place appeared in uproar as people congregated around the large wooden nursing station. Arms were flaying and voices were loud and angry as if people were growing impatient at having been forced to wait for some time for attention. It became obvious to Lucy that the masked and gowned staff weren't coping with the influx of people drifting in through the door. A young woman and her two children caught Lucy's eyes. The woman looked so sorrowful as her young infants clung to her side.

'Is it always like this?' Lucy asked Sheldon.

'Yes, I'm afraid it is at the moment, I've been informed that there's a shortage of staff caused by an outbreak of influenza in the area. You'd better come quickly this way…' he said as if they might put themselves in danger if they remained in the waiting room any longer.

Lucy glanced over her shoulder at the woman and smiled, though that did not seem appropriate, the woman smiled back and then she cuddled her children as if to comfort them. It was obvious that there was going to be a long wait for her.

'Doctor Harrington!' A shrill female voice called. Thinking it was for someone behind them, Lucy was amazed to see Sheldon in conversation with a middle-aged lady who wore a long navy dress with high white collar. 'I know you're on leave at the moment, but is there any chance you could return to duty tomorrow? As you can see, we are in the midst of a crisis here as several staff members have fallen sick with this flu outbreak.'

'Er, um..' Sheldon hesitated for a moment and she noticed his face flush pink. So, he was a doctor? Who went by the name of Harrington? How peculiar. Hadn't he mentioned on the crossing over that he used to be a journalist? Why had he never told her this before?

Sheldon turned to face Lucy, 'Please excuse me for a moment. Would you take Lady Fanshaw down that corridor there?' She nodded, now feeling unsure of things. 'Turn left at the end of the corridor and you'll see a set of wooden benches. Take a seat there and I'll be with you shortly,' he instructed.

Confused, Lucy smiled nervously at him, and led her grandmother away.

'The fellow seems quite perplexed to me!' Lady Fanshaw said suddenly, which made Lucy smile as up until now she had been unusually quiet.

'Doesn't he just?' said Lucy nodding her head in agreement.

**

Sheldon caught up with them a few minutes later, a little breathless and red-faced. 'Look, I must explain and I should have told you this before, I am a doctor at this hospital and my family name is "Harrington". I took a long leave of absence from my duties to travel to England.'

'But you're not really an author, then?' Lucy angled her head to one side, curiously.

'Yes. I am an author too and everything I told you about my book is absolutely true. You see, what I didn't tell you is that the reason I am interested in poverty is with regards to my profession and helping those who live impoverished lives. There are a few private hospitals in this area where only the rich can afford to pay for treatment, but I've been given special dispensation to research and write this book to help the poor by studying them in depth and their particular needs.'

'But what I don't understand,' said Lucy, 'is why you used your family name for your profession and a different name as an author?'

He smiled at her and placing both palms of his hands on her shoulders, said, 'It's because when the hospital board employed me here last year, they wanted me to have a different name as the author of the book, a pen name if you like. They thought if my family name of "Harrington" made it into the newspapers as the author of the book, that the hospital would attract all sorts of attention and maybe for the wrong reasons from some of the blood hound journalists. I suppose they thought it might bring the press to their doors for the wrong reasons. So, I chose the double barrelled name of "Harper Brown" as a surname instead.'

'I see,' said Lucy, though she didn't know if she really did at all.

'I don't have a lot of time to explain in depth right now as your grandmother needs attending to but I promise tonight, after supper, I shall explain everything.' That went someway to assuaging her fears. No wonder though she hadn't discovered the family name was Harrington up until now as his mother had insisted from the beginning that they all call her "Violet" and not to address her formerly. The staff referred to her as "Ma'am" and Sheldon as "Sir" so no wonder she wasn't aware of his real surname. Still, he could have explained all of this earlier to avoid confusion, she thought. And that made her feel a little uneasy, but there was no more time to dwell on it as Grandma had to be seen to.

'Now, let's take Lady Fanshaw to see Dr Meyer.' He gesticulated with his leather gloved hand to a set of double doors opposite them. He proceeded to knock, then the door was opened by a nurse who looked pristine in her blue candy-striped dress, long white apron and highly starched white cap. Lucy thought how smart she looked.

'Come this way, Lady Fanshaw,' Sheldon said, taking Grandma by the arm. Lucy thought how diminutive she looked these days, but her rheumy eyes sparkled like those of a young lady at a debutante's ball as she looked up at him.

As Lucy followed behind, she noticed how clean and clinical the room looked. Dr Meyer was sat behind his large oak desk, his bald pate shiny and bright and his mutton o'chops whiskers salt and peppered coloured to match his bushy moustache. His eyes were bright and friendly. He leapt to his feet. 'Ah, Lady Fanshaw, I've heard so much about you…' he enthused.

'But how can you have?' she giggled like a young girl, which was charming to see. Without Nurse Carmichael around, her grandmother was like a different person. And no doubt part of it was because she was off this morning's medication.

'Please forgive me. I'll explain. Doctor Harrington sent me a very long letter yesterday afternoon, explaining all. I am at your service, ma'am.'

Lady Fanshaw nodded her approval. 'Very well then as I am most definitely of lucid mind this morning, please go ahead and examine me and I give you my permission to run any necessary tests.'

Throughout the morning, she was prodded and examined by a team of doctors who asked her all sorts of questions, some Lucy had to answer for her grandmother as her memory of the situation was so hazy.

'When did you start to feel unwell?' 'What are your memories of the trip over here?' 'Are you aware of how long it took?' 'Who is the British prime minister?' 'What day is it?' On and on it went. Then there was a break for them to take coffee and biscuits where Lucy and her grandmother were left alone for twenty minutes. By then, it was half past eleven.

'I'm sorry to put you through all this, Grandma,' Lucy said, looking at the elderly lady with some concern. She was now eighty-one years old and up until last year had been relatively fit as a flea, but Lucy had witnessed the woman's deterioration at first hand.

Lucy had just finished setting their cups and saucers back down on a tray on the physician's desk when the door opened and the man himself, Dr Meyer with Sheldon behind him, both walked into the room. Sheldon closed the door and took a seat beside Lucy and Lady Fanshaw while the doctor sat behind his desk.

'I trust you are both refreshed?' He said looking at them.

'Oh, yes, thank you, Doctor,' Lucy's grandmother replied before she had a chance to slot a word in edge-wise. Lucy was so pleased at how alert her grandmother appeared to be.

'Good. Well, I've made my assessment on you and it's good news and bad news, I'm afraid, so which would you prefer first?'

Lucy felt her heart flip over but she realised they needed the bad first else they'd never concentrate on what the man was telling them, so she was relieved when her grandmother said, she wanted the bad news.

The doctor looked at Lady Fanshaw with grave concern in his eyes as Lucy held her breath. 'You're addicted to laudanum. So, we are going to have to admit you to this hospital for a while to wean you off the stuff.'

Addicted? Lucy knew her grandmother seemed reliant on the medicine but not that she couldn't do without it—so Hetty's suspicion was correct. She let out a long breath of relief. At least it was now confirmed what she had expected all along, that it was the laudanum that posed the problem for her grandmother and not some feared illness.

Lady Fanshaw just smiled. 'I thought it might be something like that,' she said. 'If the nurse has been late administering a dose, I've been feeling shaky and irritable lately.'

'And sometimes a touch of nausea and poor appetite?' Sheldon enquired.

'Yes, that too,' Lady Fanshaw agreed.

'My grandmother has lost some weight recently,' Lucy added, then she paused a moment, before asking, 'And the good news?'

'Other than that,' said Dr Meyer with a smile, 'your grandmother would have a clean bill of health. I've listened to her heart and lungs and for a woman of her age, her heart sounds strong and her lungs clear and she is also fully *compos mentis*. That is of sound mind. So, what I propose now is that we have Lady Fanshaw admitted as a private patient to the ward here. I'm sorry though that this will affect your vacation here, but you will have ample opportunity to leave for a couple of hours a day to sight see as long as you are accompanied by either a nurse or your granddaughter.'

Though not Nurse Carmichael, Lucy thought crossly.

'I'll arrange for one of the servants to bring some of your clothing here, Lady Fanshaw,' Sheldon said wisely.

'What about Grandma's nurse, though?' Lucy looked from one doctor to the other. 'I wouldn't like to think of her being involved in my grandmother's recovery.'

'Leave the nurse to me,' Sheldon smiled. 'We are short of nurses here due to the influenza outbreak, so I shall ask her if she'll join us at the casualty department and she will be paid handsomely for her time too. I'm sure given the circumstances the Board will allow it?' He looked at Dr Meyer for confirmation, who nodded his approval.

'To be fair,' Lucy said, 'I suppose she was only following orders from the family physician but why on earth would he want to keep Grandma sedated like that?'

'And what sort of age is the fellow?' Sheldon asked.

'Not much younger than you, Grandma, isn't that right?'

Lady Fanshaw nodded.

Dr Meyer cleared his throat, then looking at both ladies said, 'Maybe he's not completely au fait with modern medicine. Here in New York, we are at the heart of the medical world with all manner of innovative methods. Admittedly, some experimentation does go on, but I have witnessed for myself how advanced the medical and surgical world has now become.' Dr Meyer stroked his whiskered face.

'Some doctors though,' said Sheldon, 'are set in their ways and afraid to try anything new, but to be on the safe side, when you return to England, I would employ someone new.'

Lucy nodded. She dreaded to think what might have happened if the nurse had continued on with her doctor's orders like that. Lucy thanked her lucky stars that she'd encountered Sheldon on the ship and for more than the reason of her grandmother's health, for her own welfare too. She owed him a debt of gratitude, that much was evident.

Chapter Thirteen

1874

"Home Again"

The journey to Huntington Hall seemed never ending as the coach rattled over cobbled roads and dips in dirt tracks and ruts in country pathways. Archie felt as though his guts were being shook inside out. He was upset enough as it was knowing that something had happened to Uncle Walter, so when Mrs Brewster dipped her hand into her wicker basket and unwrapped a muslin cloth to offer him a hunk of bread and a slice of cheese on the journey, he held up his hand and politely refused.

'Never mind, Archie,' she soothed. 'Perhaps you'll feel like a little something later on?' She raised her brows in expectation.

He smiled and nodded, though he knew he wouldn't feel like anything at all until he'd seen for himself just how Uncle Walter was.

Strange, it was only a few short weeks ago that he'd come this way with him to attend the school and now he was returning and unable to take in any of the sights along the way.

As the coach drew up outside Huntingdon Hall, his stomach suddenly lurched and Mrs Brewster's hand lightly touched his. 'Be brave, lad,' she said.

He nodded as tears filled his eyes. Mrs Stockley the Cook, and Polly the kitchen maid, were waiting for him as he ascended the coach, both having serious expressions on their faces. He gulped as he walked towards them. Immediately he was in Cook's arms and being cuddled against her large bosom. Then Polly wittered on about how great it was to see him again. She jabbered on and on, saying didn't he look a right little lord an' all in all his posh garb. It felt to him, as though his Uncle Walter should be there to greet him, but of course, he wasn't.

'My uncle...' was all he managed to say as Cook held him tightly to her bosom so he felt barely able to breathe. It wasn't usual form for servants to hug family members at the house but in this case, Archie had no one else to do so.

Much to his relief, Cook released him and holding him at arms' length to peer into his eyes said, 'The doctor is with your uncle right now. He's sustained a head injury. We thought we'd better get you here...' then she lowered her voice to barely a whisper, 'just in case...'

Just in case of what?

'By heck, lad, you look shell shocked,' said Polly. 'And ain't you going to introduce us?' Her sharp eyes took in the form of Mrs Brewster.

As no reply was forthcoming from Archie the woman introduced herself. 'I'm Mrs Brewster. I work at Compton Manor School and I'll need to return shortly. I just came to accompany Archie on his journey.'

'And most right it is an' all,' said Cook smiling, her blue eyes twinkling with warmth. 'I daresay you and the coach driver will come inside for a cuppa?'

Mrs Brewster smiled and nodded, overcome by such kindness. 'Thank you. That would be most welcome. But what am I to report back to Mr Criddlington?'

'Who's that when he's at home?' Asked Polly.

'Mind your lip, gal!' Cook shot her a glance, and then turning to Mrs Brewster said, 'I'll tell you all you need to know when you come into the warmth inside.'

***

It was another long hour before Archie was allowed to see his uncle. The housekeeper, Mrs Linley, led him up the stairs. For once she wasn't so stiff and starchy. 'How are you getting along at your new school, Master Pomfrey?' She asked. It was almost as though she had a new found respect for him since he'd taken that name on.

'Very well, thank you, Mrs Linley,' he replied. On no account did he want to tell her of some of the goings on there. If he was going to confide in anyone it would be Cook, Polly or even Mr Featherstone, the gardener. He trusted all of them, but Mrs Linley he did not. Though it wasn't as if she'd done anything to him as such, he supposed the reason was because she hadn't been that friendly towards him the first time she'd ever met him, and in his book, people usually showed their true colours within minutes of meeting him. He'd learned that on the streets of Whitechapel. He'd immediately known Bill Brackley the evil chimney sweep was a bad 'un. As soon as he set eyes on him, he'd trembled.

As they reached the top of the stairs and went to approach his uncle's bedroom, Mrs Linley looked at him with compassion in her eyes. 'The master's all right physically,' she explained to him, 'but mentally he's not quite the same as to how you remember him...'

Archie didn't understand.

Sensing his bewilderment, she said, 'He's now prone to mood swings us staff have discovered. He gets angered easily and seems to have difficulty in recalling our names. The doctor says he thinks it's a temporary issue, not a permanent one, so I'm just warning for your own sake as I realise how sensitive you are, Archibald.'

Archie felt her words rankle him. Sensitive indeed! If he was so ruddy sensitive how come he managed to survive on the streets? That woman was still getting under his skin.

She knocked gently on the door to hear a woman's voice call, 'Please enter.'

'He has a nurse now,' Mrs Linley whispered as she gave Archie a gentle push inside.

Seeing Uncle Walter lying in bed looking so grey and frail, pulled him up sharply. His uncle looked at him and for a moment there was a flicker of recognition. 'Aren't you Alicia's boy, Archie?' he croaked.

'Y...yes, sir,' Archie replied feeling a little fearful.

'Then where is she?' he asked peering at the door.

'Who, Uncle Walter?'

'Your mother of course! Isn't she with you?'

Archie glanced at the housekeeper for reassurance, who after a moment's pause said, 'Your sister isn't here at the moment, your nephew has come alone, sir!'

Why on earth was Mrs Linley lying to her uncle? Everyone knew his mother was dead! And why was Uncle Walter acting as if his own sister was still alive?

'Come here then, Archie?' his uncle said, his voice sounding louder now. Oh dear, was this the anger that Mrs Linley spoke of?

Timidly, Archie made his way towards the man's bed.

'And what brought you here today?' he asked, now with a smile on his face. Much to Archie's relief.

Archie cleared his throat. 'I came from school as I received a message to say you'd had an accident, Uncle Walter.'

'Oh that, it was nothing,' he said.

Archie looked at Mrs Linley who shrugged, then averted her eyes.

His uncle suddenly sat himself up in bed as if to take interest. 'What school are you in these days, then, young man?'

But you know which school, you arranged it for me.

Mrs Linley shot him a warning glance.

'Compton Manor, sir.'

His uncle's eyes enlarged. 'Jolly good show. I went there for a term but I was expelled…'

But you've already told me that!

He said nothing about it, just listened to his uncle prattle on about the school and go off on various tangents about topics that made no sense at all to him. It was difficult for Archie not to break down in tears, so upset by this was he. Maybe Mrs Linley was right after all about his sensitivity.

As if realising how upset Archie was, Mrs Linley looked at him and said softly, 'I think it's best your uncle has some rest now, Archie.'

He nodded and bade Uncle Walter farewell. Then he ran out into the garden and began sobbing profusely. This really was a lot for him to take in. After weeks of being away from home and enduring some of the things he'd had to at the school, it had all finally got too much for him. He was now accepted by the other boys in the dorm but it had been hard work for him to get to that stage.

'Hey, what's up, young Archie!' he heard a man's voice call.

He turned to see Mr Featherstone stood before him, wheelbarrow in hand and tobacco pipe in mouth, his old tweed jacket worn over a woollen shirt and a pair of corduroy breeches tied at the knees with pieces of string. Immediately he ran towards him as tears streamed down his cheeks. It was so reassuring to see the elderly man once again.

The gardener dropped his wheelbarrow and hugged Archie. 'There, there. Don't take on so. Tell me what's been happening?' The man's voice soothed him and Archie found the faint whiff of the tobacco fumes on his clothing comforting somehow. He was home at last.

'It's…m…my uncle,' he sobbed. 'I don't think he really remembers me properly since his accident. Well, he does sort of remember me but it's like how he knew me before I came to live at the house. He's very distant and thinks my mother is still alive.'

Mr Featherstone released him from his embrace. 'Oh, I see…' he said thoughtfully taking a long puff on his pipe. 'Now then, I reckon it's like this, you see. Your Uncle Walter hit his head and then he lost consciousness, from what Cook told me. Now when you think about it, if he hit his head then maybe it's jumbled up his thoughts. If he rests a while longer, then all them messy thoughts will slot back into place, you'll see.'

Archie began to smile. It was a simple explanation that made a lot of sense to him. 'Do you really think so, Mr Featherstone?' he asked enthusiastically.

'Aye, I really do, Archie. Now help me push this wheelbarrow of old cuttings over to the greenhouse, son. Then we'll have some homemade ginger beer. Greta made it for me,' he said proudly.

Greta? Who on earth was she?

Spotting his confusion, Mr Featherstone laughed heartily. 'Cook, or Mrs Stockley to you,' he said.

Before he'd gone away, he'd noticed the pair were becoming fond of one another. Come to think of it Cook had often called the man into the kitchen to give him a large helping of one of her pies or puds. He guessed the pair were kind of lonely and good companions for one other.

***

Life back at the house was strange to say the least as over the following days, Archie started to become used to it. There were no more meals sitting in the dining room with his uncle as the man spent his days in bed, slipping in and out of lucidity. Had the school allowed him back here in case he died? It was almost the end of term anyhow and soon he would have had to come home. He'd written a letter to Lucy, explaining the situation, but so far there'd been no reply and no matter how nice Cook and Polly were to him, he felt lost.

So, it came as a great surprise to him one day when a carriage drew up at the door and Lucy stepped out of it. She did look a right little lady and all in her green velvet dress with matching cape and fur trimmed bonnet—the weather had got a lot colder of late. He could have sworn she'd grown a couple of inches since he'd seen her last.

He went running down the steps to greet her and swung her around excitedly in his arms. 'Oh Lucy, this is such a surprise!' He enthused with a lump in his throat as the tears of joy threatened to spill down his cheeks.

'I'm so sorry about everything that's happened, Archie,' she said blinking in the faint afternoon sun. 'I was away in the Lake District with Mama and Mr Knight. So, I only just received your letter on my return, so I dashed over to see you. How is your uncle now?'

'And I'm so glad you came. He's not right, Lucy. He seems to get muddled up and confused. I think sometimes he even forgets who I am.'

'That's dreadful.' She sighed. 'And what about your school? Have you settled in there?'

He nodded. 'Eventually, though it was hard at first. They were a cliquey lot but I have two best friends there.'

Was that a frown he saw on her face or was he imagining things? Then he realised what he'd said. 'But of course, you are my very best friend and always will be.'

She beamed and let out a long sigh of relief. 'For a moment there, I thought you'd forgotten all about me!'

'Where are my manners? Come inside and we'll take afternoon tea together! That's if you haven't eaten as yet?'

She shook her head. 'Oh no. I've been too excited since reading your letter!'

'That's settled then, I'll order a plate of sandwiches and cakes for us and some of Cook's lemonade!'

She smiled at him as she seemed to be as pleased to see him as he was to see her. And what a change it was and all to be in the company of such a pretty young girl instead of some of those ruffians back at Compton Manor School.

***

Days settled very much into a pattern of Archie breakfasting alone in the dining room, where he scanned the newspapers as his uncle usually had. Although a lot of what he read was boring, some of it was of interest to him. The current affairs mentioned opened up his mind to what was going on in the world at the present time. Old Penny had been the one to remind him it was good to read all manner of things to open up his mind. He'd just read that a School of Medicine had opened in London, just for women to train as doctors. Fancy that! Apparently, it would be the very first medical school in the whole of Britain to train women. He'd have to remember to tell Lucy about that.

Following breakfast, he decided he'd go to help Mr Featherstone in the garden as the man was full of rheumatism now, and although he did his best, Archie thought his uncle would do well to employ a new young gardener to help the fellow.

The rest of the day he'd spend walking in the grounds, skimming stones across the lake, climbing trees and looking at birds' nests, though he never removed any eggs, but he liked to sketch them and record them in his leather notepad and try to find out what breed a particular bird was. It kept him occupied until the times when he could see Lucy again.

He kept himself fit too, skipping with an old rope and running around the lake because as far as he was concerned, since taking the boxing lessons which had boosted his confidence, he decided that when he did return to school after the holiday, he would never, ever allow Ashcroft or anyone else to bully him again. Breathlessly, he ran through the woods, arriving at the back door of the kitchen, to see Cook stood there with a large silver salver with a big roast ham on it. 'Yer just in time, Archie,' she enthused, 'guess what?'

He shrugged his shoulders. Was she going to tell him the moon was made of green cheese or something?

'It's yer uncle,' Polly popped out from behind Cook, causing Cook to give her a sideward glance at having stolen her thunder for a moment. As if realising this, Polly kept quiet for Cook to have her moment of glory.

'Well, the doctor has just left and he says the master has made great strides and is now starting to remember things. He's asking to see you, Archie,' she said enthusiastically.

'That's great,' said Archie, 'I'll just get washed and changed and go to see him.'

'Don't keep him too long not to tire him out though,' Cook warned.

'I won't!' He replied brightly.

He was just about to dash through the kitchen when Polly grabbed hold of his arm. 'Hey, I swear you've grown a couple of inches since I last saw you, lad!' she said. 'Hasn't he, Mrs Stockley?'

Cook nodded. 'He has an' all. It's all this good food he's been getting here since he's been back home. Fuel for him.'

Cook might well have been right but he also put it down to all the exercise he'd been getting and the fact he was growing older. He'd noticed his voice growing croaky lately and he knew soon he'd start to sprout some whiskers. Mr Featherstone had told him that.

Feeling pleased with himself, he made his way to his bedroom to wash and change.

***

Uncle Walter was seated in a wing backed armchair by his bedroom window when he arrived, it was so good to see him out of bed. 'Archie!' he said with a big smile on his face.

Archie smiled back at him. 'So, you're feeling a lot better then, Uncle Walter? How are you?'

'Never mind about me, dear boy. How are you getting on at Compton Manor School?'

Archie breathed a sigh of relief, at last his uncle remembered where he'd been recently. 'Not so bad. It was hard settling in at first but now I get on with almost everyone there,' he replied in a cheerful manner.

His uncle nodded. 'It will make a man of you. You've already lasted longer than I did, I'm so proud of you. Tonight, if you don't mind, we'll dine together in my bedroom. Then Nurse assures me in a couple of days I can join you downstairs in the dining room. Is that permissible?' He quirked a questioning brow.

Permissible? It was positively wonderful. 'I'd very much like that,' said Archie, nodding in agreement.

And so over the following days and weeks, Uncle Walter regained his health and strength, much to Archie's relief. He'd have hated to have lost the only relative he had left in the world and soon it would be time to return to boarding school.

Chapter Fourteen

1885

"Parting is Such Sweet Sorrow"

It was strange leaving her grandmother behind at the hospital but Lucy realised she was leaving the woman in good hands after being assured that Eastvale Community Hospital was one of the best in the area.

As Lucy, Hetty, and Sheldon entered his house, Nurse Carmichael stood there, arms folded with narrowed gaze. 'I'd very much like to know what happened to my charge?' she said through pursed lips.

Sheldon smiled. 'Your charge, ma'am, has been admitted to a local community hospital. There she will be given extra special care for her addiction to the laudanum you have been plying her with!' His voice rose with each word and Lucy could tell he meant every one of them.

The nurse's eyes widened as she held up her arms in defence as she took a step back. 'B...but I was only following Doctor Hamley's orders,' she protested, then she swallowed hard as if she realised she was now on shaky ground.

'That may be so,' Sheldon persisted, 'but were you not concerned that Lady Fanshaw was becoming so sleepy and disorientated? And her granddaughter says she has lost a dreadful amount of body weight too as she now has very little appetite after imbibing all that medication you've been pouring down her throat! In fact, I would go as far as to say she is a shadow of her former self thanks to you!'

Enid Carmichael lowered her eyelids and began to tremble.

That's shame that is, Lucy thought. Also, possible fear of Sheldon's anger.

The nurse took in a deep breath of composure. 'Well, I, er, yes. But I thought maybe sleeping was part of the cure?' She looked Sheldon squarely in the eyes with her chin tilted upwards in an act of defiance.

'If you thought that then maybe, Madam, you need further training. From now on, you won't be caring for her ladyship, instead you shall, for the remainder of your time here, work at the Eastvale Community Hospital…'

The nurse's mouth popped open then snapped shut again.

'And,' continued Sheldon, 'you will do so for the remainder of your visit here.'

'But whose orders are these? Who are you to tell me what to do?' Enid's hands went up in horror as she showed her vertical palms as if about to defend herself, but she was no match for Sheldon when he was in this sort of mood.

'Actually,' Lucy pointed out, 'Sheldon is a doctor at the hospital himself, I've only just discovered this.'

Enid Carmichael harrumphed loudly.

'A surgeon actually,' Sheldon said, glancing at Lucy with a twinkle in his eyes.

'That might be as maybe but I still ask who has directed this change of plan?' Enid waited for a suitable answer to her question as a long, uncomfortable silence enveloped them all.

Hetty, who had been standing shyly in the background, bravely stepped forward and looking the nurse in the eyes said, 'Her ladyship has. She agrees with every single word too, an' all!'

Enid's eyes seemed to take on a beady looking quality as she glared at the girl and rose her arm above her head as if about to bring it down quickly to strike her, causing Hetty to step back in horror. 'No, you don't, yer old witch!' she yelled at the woman.

'Stop this at once!' Sheldon shouted, causing Lucy to tremble, she'd never heard him raise his voice before. 'Nurse Carmichael, you are to do as you are told or else find your own passage back to England.'

The nurse's bottom lip trembled. 'But I don't have the money to do so…I can't afford it.' For a moment, Lucy thought the woman was about to cry as her bottom lip trembled and her eyes glazed over. No doubt she feared that even if she could scrape together enough money for her passage, she'd end up stowing away in steerage with people of a lowlier class than herself.

'Then until it is time for Lady Fanshaw to return home to England herself, you must obey her orders. After all, it is the lady herself who is paying you and not the doctor. And from what I've heard of him, he sounds an unquestionable quack to me! Now, I'll hear no more of this. We shall all dine shortly in the dining room and you are to report to the head nurse at the hospital first thing in the morning. You shall reside on the premises in the nurses' quarters there until further notice. There's been an outbreak of influenza in the area, so the hospital needs all the help it can get. You shall be paid handsomely for your services along with your allowance from the lady. Now that can't be all bad, can it?'

Enid's eyes filled with tears as she turned and ran from the room, staggering along the way. Sheldon's words had hit hard, upsetting the woman greatly, but in Lucy's eyes, she needed pulling down a peg or two anyhow. She looked at him with admiration.

'I suppose I might have been a little harsh there for a moment,' he ran his hand over his moustache as if mulling things over.

'No, I don't think you were at all, Sheldon. She needed telling and now, thanks to you, I have the assurance of my grandmother's health and safety. As if on cue, Hetty slipped out of the room. Sheldon drew up close and looked deep into Lucy's eyes as he stroked her cheek. 'Tomorrow, I shall return to work earlier than expected as I am needed, but tonight, after we dine, would you do me the honour of accompanying me to the opera?'

'Oh, yes please,' Lucy gasped as her heart raced from his close encounter. Years ago, something like accompanying a gentleman to the opera would have fazed her, but Mama had taught her the finer things in life and she knew all the songs from the great operas. But she didn't much care if it turned out to be one she'd seen before. It would provide her with the chance to dress up in one of her best gowns that she'd brought with her and look her best for the evening, and even more importantly, to spend time alone with Sheldon.

Lucy's heart hammered in expectation with the excitement of it all.

Sheldon smiled at her. 'It might be my last chance to let my hair down as it will now be safer for me to stay at the hospital for a while instead of coming back and forth to the house and possibly spreading disease. You are still welcome to stay here of course.'

She nodded wistfully as she turned to gaze out of the window. It was now twilight, that strange time of day when it was neither dark nor light and objects made silhouettes against the landscape. 'Thank you,' she said gratefully, as she carried on staring outside. It wasn't so long ago when she would have been making plans for the future with Archie. Hadn't he begged her to marry him once upon a time? But then not shown up when she was due to leave England? He'd let her down badly at the final hour. She had toyed with writing him a long letter, not to ask where he'd been but to share her news just to maintain contact, but now she feared that all was best left well alone, at least for time being and Sheldon was just the man to keep her mind off things.

***

The following morning as dawn broke, Lucy lay in her bed day dreaming about the marvellous evening they'd enjoyed. She'd felt like a princess stepping out of Sheldon's carriage and into the beautiful Grand City Opera House. There had even been someone waiting to assist with parking up Sheldon's carriage. Once inside the entrance, she surveyed its plush deep velvet embossed wallpaper, thick scarlet carpets, lush green potted aspidistra and Kentai palm plants and overhead, the fancy gasoliers suspended from the ceiling. She drew in a deep breath of awe. What luxury. They were both greeted by a lady who took her fur wrap and showed them to their seats. And once the murmuring crowd were all seated, a hush had descended upon the place as the red velvet curtains drew back to reveal the performers on stage. Lucy was delighted when she discovered that it was the opera *Carmen* being performed as it was one opera she'd never seen with Mama.

She jolted back to reality as she heard echoing footsteps on the landing as she lay in her bed. Enid Carmichael preparing to leave for the hospital, no doubt. Sheldon had said a carriage would be waiting outside to transport her there and he'd be leaving in it with her. She put on her dressing gown and watched from the landing window as the pair clambered inside the carriage. Enid looked paler than usual and Lucy guessed she'd had little or no sleep, whereas Sheldon looked bright and active. She'd said her goodbyes to him last night after they'd returned from the opera house and he'd taken her in his arms outside the front door. She'd sworn to him that she'd take care of his mother too while he was away. And then he'd brought his lips crashing down on hers for a kiss so full of passion, it left her heady with desire for him. How was she supposed to get through the next couple of weeks after that kiss and no Sheldon around the house? It was going to be hard for them both, she supposed, but she understood that the hospital needed him more than she did right now.

Lucy kept herself busy for the rest of the day pottering around the large house and was becoming embedded in her own thoughts when she sensed someone behind her. She turned to see Sheldon's mother.

'You look so lost there, my dear,' she said, her eyes showing warmth and compassion.

'I was thinking about my grandmother,' Lucy said softly.

'Come and take afternoon tea with me in the drawing room,' the woman quirked her silver brow in expectation.

'I'd love to, thank you, Mrs...'

'Please, I don't particularly like formalities. I thought I'd already made it clear you can call me Violet,' she said smiling.

As they sat in the drawing room, Lucy couldn't help warming to the woman who reminded her so much of home with her English accent. She was so down to earth too for someone so wealthy.

'You look a little puzzled there, Lucy?' Violet drew her brows together as if puzzled herself.

'I was just wondering where Sheldon's father is?' Lucy had said the words before she was ready to and now sat there in horror. What would the lady think of her?

But instead the woman smiled. 'That's all right, dear, you are at liberty to ask. I fell in love with Sheldon's father when I was a young lady living in Hampshire, England. We married and he wanted to emigrate to America, so we moved here and Sheldon was born but unfortunately, his father, Tom, was killed in an accident.'

'Oh, I am so sorry,' Lucy said, now wishing she hadn't asked.

'It's all right, it was a long time ago, Sheldon was just a few years old when it happened. His father was run over by the wheels of a coach and unfortunately, Sheldon witnessed it happening as he was with his father at the time.' Violet's eyes filled with tears.

'That must have had a profound effect on him?'

'Oh, it did. Most definitely. It was that one incident that made him passionate about becoming a doctor.' She paused a moment to take a deep breath in and exhaled as if letting some of the sadness she was experiencing out once again. 'You see, there was a doctor in attendance at the time, he had witnessed the whole thing from the street opposite and was the first on the scene. He battled to save my Tom, but alas, it was too late. He had been about to amputate a limb when he thought my husband died from the shock of it all.' She brought her knuckles to her mouth as she closed her eyes in remembrance of the horrible incident.

'It must have been truly dreadful for you both.' Lucy offered the woman her clean, lace handkerchief, which she took and dabbed at her eyes.

'So, Sheldon vowed from that time on that he would get the best grades at school so he could train to become a doctor, and do you know what?'

Lucy quirked a brow. 'No?'

'He kept to that promise. Previously he had coasted along at school, but when he set his mind to it, he worked hard, so much harder than his peers and gained all the top grades. No one could reach him. But alas, it all came at a cost as he lost friends over it as they saw him as being this snotty young man who had no time for other activities but they didn't realise the truth of it all.'

'I see,' said Lucy, laying her hand on top of the woman's more gnarled, crepe-like one. 'And now?'

'And now…he is known for being one of the finest surgeons that New York has to offer. He was head hunted for The Eastvale Community hospital by Doctor Meyer, the doctor who examined your grandmother.'

'Really?' Lucy felt surprised about that. 'That's wonderful but when I first encountered Sheldon aboard that ship, he led me to believe he was only a writer?'

'Well he is really, writing is his passion, he keeps a regular journal and other such things.'

Lucy nodded, guessing that Sheldon's mother didn't like to show off about him as an author and was playing it all down. She obviously didn't wish to mention his journalistic background nor the book he'd written. How sweet of her. No doubt, he didn't boast about it himself to her.

Lucy smiled, she thought she was beginning to get a better picture of Sheldon, the man who had stolen her heart.

Chapter Fifteen

1874

"Conquered at Last"

Back at school, Archie was greeted warmly by his peers, who all wanted to know how his long absence away from the school had been. Carruthers and Wally even loitered around outside waiting for him when his carriage drew up that morning. There was one person though who wasn't pleased to see him and by his haughty air and the dangerous gleam in his eye when he caught sight of Archie, it was evident he would now make his life hell. That boy was Ashcroft, who now seemed a little shorter though. It was then, Archie realised with some pride that it wasn't the boy who had got shorter, as how could that possibly happen anyhow? It was he, Archie Pomfrey, who had sprouted up by a couple of inches. And wasn't it Cook and Polly who had noticed and all?

Puffed up with pride, Archie strutted into the dorm where the boys couldn't wait to pat him on the back and share their tucker with him. Archie didn't intend eating too many pork pies or sweet sponge cakes though. He became more determined than ever that he was now going to teach Ashcroft the lesson of his life. To do so, would mean keeping himself trim. So, it would be back to boxing lessons for him and maybe a few runs around the lake a week. It wasn't just for his sake though that he wanted to get the better of the boy, it was for other lads at the school, younger ones he'd seen Ashcroft bullying. If he wasn't trying to trip them up in the corridors, then he was cuffing them around the ears and making them cry. And the teachers were turning a blind eye to it because as a six former, he was granted certain privileges like sending young boys on errands and disciplining them for misdemeanours when members of teaching staff were not around.

Early one afternoon, he found a young boy sobbing in the school grounds. The boy was so upset that his shoulders were heaving and he was finding it hard to catch his breath. 'What's the matter?' Archie said gently as he studied the boy's distraught face.

'N…nothing,' came the shuddering reply.

It was obvious that something had gone on but this lad was too frightened to speak out.

'Look,' whispered Archie, glancing around him to ensure they weren't being watched. When he was satisfied that all was well, he said, 'you don't have to name the brute who did this to you but my guess is it was Ashcroft? Just nod if that is the case, I shan't drop you in it.'

The boy stopped crying and nodded. Archie handed him a clean handkerchief from his own jacket pocket so that he could dry his snot filled face. 'I thought as much. Here, wipe your eyes and nose with that not to show anyone else what's happened. I shall deal with this. For Pete's sake tell me what he did to you?'

The lad, who was very small for his age as a first former, looked at Archie with a great deal of trust in his eyes. 'H…he sent for me to go to his dorm and then he…he…kept swinging me around. He tied me to the bed and removed my shoes and socks and began bringing a hot poker to my feet from the fireplace.'

'He what?' said Archie angrily. 'Did he burn you then?'

'No,' the boy shook his head and looked at the ground. Then he brought his eyes to meet with Archie's. 'No, but several times he held it close to the soles of my feet, the threat was enough to scare me though. And I wet my trousers with fright. He just laughed at me...' He began to cry once again.

Archie gritted his teeth and balled his hands into fists. 'And why did he do that, do you think?'

Fresh tears filled the boy's eyes. 'He's been taking money from me and my tucker too when it's given to me. Last week he stole my pork pie and the week before, an apple tart our cook had baked especially for me.'

For some reason, hearing about the food felt worse to Archie than hearing about the money being taken. They didn't get to spend much money being in boarding school, except for the rare times they were allowed into the village, but taking someone's favourite food sent from home was sacrilege in his eyes.

'What's your name?'

'Bart,' the boy said shyly.

'Now look here, Bart, this isn't going to go on much longer, believe me. If he accosts you again, I will be ready and waiting.' Archie had begun to formulate a plan and he couldn't wait to get started on it. 'Now dry those eyes, go back to the dorm while the others are still having their lunch and change those wet trousers, so no one need ever know. You can rinse them quickly in one of the sinks and put them to dry on a radiator. By the time lessons are over today, they'll be dry once again. You do have a spare pair, don't you?'

The boy nodded, gratefully.

'Good,' Archie said. 'Now run along. This won't go on much longer...'

The boy thanked him and Archie stood there watching him running back to the grey building. With any luck, none of the others in his class would know what a humiliating experience he'd just endured.

Later, when Archie related the incident to Carruthers and Wally, they were all ears about Archie's revenge, but he decided to leave the lad's name out of it. 'But do you really think you're up to taking on Ashcroft?' Wally asked, his eyes appearing large and interested behind his round spectacles.

'I shan't know until I try it out. I'm getting quite good at boxing now and quick on my feet.'

'But he's taller than you,' Carruthers said with a concerned look on his face.

'Not that much taller anymore and I bet I can outrun the brute any day!'

Both boys smiled as if they didn't doubt it.

'He's a bully who's been taking tucker and money from younger boys, especially if they look scared of him,' Archie said. 'That's why I intend giving him a taste of his own medicine.'

'But how do you intend doing that?' Wally quirked an interested brow.

Archie tapped the side of his nose with his index finger. 'Just you wait and see,' he said. 'Just you wait and see.'

***

A couple of weeks later, when Archie had ensured he was at his prime fitness wise, he left the dorm under the cover of darkness, the rest of the boys were fast asleep in their beds, Wally snoring as his chest moved up and down beneath the covers. Carruthers turned over in his bed and on seeing what Archie was up to, insisted on going with him.

'Please don't wake the others,' Archie whispered as he watched the boy quickly slip on his dressing gown and slide into his carpet slippers. Archie was already dressed in his training clothing from the boxing gym.

Once down the landing and out through the back door they made their way to the sixth form dormitory which was three storeys above them as they walked. There was no sign of life from inside except for a couple of lanterns lit on the landing windows which gave the place an eerie impression of flickering lights and scary shadows.

'But what do you intend doing?' Carruthers asked.

'I'm going to throw up some stones to Ashcroft's window to nab his attention. Now, what I want you to do is to cover for me. When he answers tell him that somehow you've got locked out. Pretend to cry as he'll see that as a sign of weakness.'

Carruthers gulped as if not realising what he was letting himself in for. 'All right,' he finally said in a tone of reluctance.

Archie slapped his back. 'I knew you wouldn't let me down. Now while you're drawing him outside, I'll be hiding behind the bushes. Got it?'

Carruthers nodded as if unconvinced that the plan would work.

Archie knelt down to pick up a couple of small stones from the ground and chipped them at Ashcroft's window. He stood back and hid behind a bush. At first there was no response, but then he threw another and took cover once again to hear the sash window pushed open with a thud. Ashcroft stood there poking his head out. He drowsily asked, 'You boy, what's going on there?'

'Please, Ashcroft,' said Carruthers in a whining voice, 'I'm locked out. Can you help me get back to my dorm?'

'No, I certainly cannot, you little scroat!' Ashcroft scoffed. He was about to slam the window shut.

Thinking that maybe now Carruthers would give up, Archie was surprised to hear him say, 'Please Ashcroft, I've got plenty of tucker delivered from home, you can have your pick next time I'm allowed some.'

Ashcroft stopped what he was doing and poked his head back out of the window, growing quiet for a while as if mulling things over in his mind. 'Tucker you say?'

'Yes.'

'Any money as well?'

'Only the birthday money my aunt gave me…'

Archie chuckled to himself, that would surely lure Ashcroft to come downstairs.

'Very well, I'll be right there now!' He shouted back in a chirpy fashion.

Archie and Carruthers began to giggle.

A couple of minutes later, Ashcroft appeared at the back door in his flannel dressing gown and slippers. His normally neat hair sprouting out at all angles. He yawned loudly, and then, once drawing up to Carruthers he had a certain look on his face that Archie didn't much care for as he saw him grab Carruthers by the collar of his dressing gown and shake him roughly. 'You bet I'll have your tucker and your birthday money too. How much did your aunt give you?' he demanded to know.

'N…not sure…' Carruther's voice sounded weak and shaky causing Archie to emerge from behind the bush to face the brute. Now almost as tall as him, they stood eye to eye.

'Let go of him, you bullying bugger!' Archie yelled.

A big smile appeared on Ashcroft's face. 'Two scroats!' He chuckled as he proceeded to grab hold of Archie's collar with the other hand, but he was too swift for him and ducked out of the way. He was used to ducking and diving during his boxing lessons.

Astonished that the lad had got the better of him, Ashcroft released Carruthers, who fell to the ground with a bump. The disorientated boy roughly pulled himself up on a low nearby stone wall to compose himself. Ashcroft wasn't interested in him anymore, now he was far more interested in the boy dancing around him with his fists raised in challenge.

Ashcroft could hardly contain himself as he laughed so loud that his echoing voice into the night air, brought several of his peers to their bedroom windows to see what was going on. Sash windows were heard sliding open, one by one.

'Give him what for Ashcroft!' and 'Fight! Fight! There's a fight!' the boys shouted. And, at the sound of those cries, even more boys began poking their heads out of the windows to get a good view at the sport taking place down below.

Ashcroft brought his fists into a fighting pose and began to jab at Archie. He hadn't bargained for this, he hadn't realised the boy could box, but Archie was fast on his feet and furious. He managed to swerve out of the way each time. In frustration, Ashcroft brought his fist up in an uppercut punch to his chin, which sent Archie flying into the bushes as the older boys laughed. Ashcroft turned to look up at them and then smiling thinking he had got the better of Archie, began to walk back to the dorm with hands held high in a pose of triumph, until he heard, 'Stay and fight, you coward!' from behind him. Archie was back on his feet and ready for more, this time he was determined not to get caught out.

Immediately, the smile was wiped from Ashcroft's face as he turned to face Archie. He wasn't prepared for this.

'Let him have it, Ashy!' Someone shouted from an upstairs window.

'Leave it be now, don't be so silly,' Carruthers hissed. 'You'll get hurt!'

'No,' said Archie firmly. 'I have got to stand my ground.'

Shaking his head, Carruthers stepped back, obviously not wanting to find himself in the firing line.

Then Ashcroft lashed out, his reach a little longer than Archie's, but the boy was too quick for him as he ducked to miss the punch and danced around the bully. His aim was to tire the lad out. Each time Ashcroft missed a punch, Archie felt his confidence soar and he heard Carruthers giggle behind him, now getting into the spirit of things.

A few minutes later, Archie managed to land a punch on Ashcroft's chin and knocked him spark out to the ground.

There was a yell from an upstairs window as the older boys came running to check on him.

'Let's get out of here!' Carruthers yelled as Archie stood there momentarily rooted to the spot. Jolting back to reality, as the adrenalin started to pump around his body, Archie found his feet and flew after his friend. He'd be in trouble for this, no doubt. Back at the dorm gasping for breath, he crawled beneath the covers, exhausted and aching from top to toe. He dreaded what would happen tomorrow: would he get expelled for his actions or just end up with a rap on the knuckles? Maybe one act of bravery would bring his reputation into disrepute both at the school and with his uncle back home.

Chapter Sixteen

1885

"A Reunion"

It was a full ten days later when Sheldon returned home to the house. In all that time, Lucy found herself growing close to his mother as they spent time going for long walks in the gardens of the house, taking afternoon tea and embroidering cloths on the back veranda afterwards. She was becoming very fond of the middle-aged woman and could tell from the wistful look in her cornflower blue eyes when she spoke of England sometimes that she missed home even though she had a beautiful house in Auburn. Reading between the lines, Lucy guessed she'd felt this way since the death of her husband.

Lucy had missed Sheldon dreadfully during this time but she realised he was needed at the hospital.

Later that afternoon, the front door opened suddenly and Sheldon breezed into the house, his face flushed and with an excited glint in his eyes, he announced, 'It's on the decline!' Violet drew her eyebrows together in puzzlement as he placed his black leather Gladstone bag down in the hallway. He removed his scarf and bowler hat into the arms of an awaiting maid, then drew closer to the pair.

'What is?' Lucy blinked.

'The influenza out break. The casualty numbers have now peaked and cases are falling, that's why I'm back home and I've brought someone with me...'

Silhouetted in the doorway was Grandmother. Lucy hadn't seen her looking so well for a long time. 'Grandma!' she shouted and she ran to embrace the woman. 'You look so much better,' she said taking a step back to appraise the woman's appearance.

'Oh, I am. I'm well rested too.' She smiled and then kissed Lucy's cheek. Over the years, Lucy had noticed how much more affectionate her grandmother had become and she supposed that might have been because when she'd first met her, the reason she'd kept her at arms' length was because she was still grieving for the daughter she mistakenly thought she'd lost forever.

'Your grandmother was well looked after,' Sheldon explained. 'She was put on a nourishing diet. Thankfully, there are no more harmful drugs in her system.' His eyes caught Lucy's. 'Maybe we can have a chat later?' He dropped his voice a notch.

She nodded, wondering what he had to tell her. Looking past him towards the doorway, she asked, 'Is Nurse Carmichael with you?'

He shook his head. 'She's still working at the hospital. She'll probably return here next week, hopefully having learned her lesson. Though, I have to say she is a boon at the hospital. She's been put in charge of one of the respiratory wards and has all the young nurses running around in circles to get things done. Before she was on that ward, standards had slipped as the matron herself had been taken ill with the flu and her stand-in was rather slip shod, so I'm informed.'

Lucy beamed, secretly happy that Nurse Carmichael had at long last found her vocation. Her breath caught in her chest as Sheldon laid his hand on her arm. 'I'm just going to freshen up before dinner,' he said, shooting her a charming smile.

Violet's eyes watered and Lucy wondered were those unshed tears of relief she was holding back because she was pleased to see her only son safely back home? She had, after all, expressed her fears about the flu outbreak to Lucy earlier as they'd sat chatting in the garden, or were those tears of sadness as her son reminded her of his father? Lucy had seen the painting of Thomas that hung in the drawing room. Father and son were very alike except that Sheldon's father had sported mutton chop style whiskers, whereas Sheldon was clean shaven apart from a thin pencil style moustache. Ironically, from what Violet had told her, Sheldon was now approaching the age his father had been when he'd departed from this world. Maybe she'd feared losing him too when he was working at such a critical time at the hospital and might have endangered his own health in the process.

Before dinner, Lucy sat on the back porch with Lady Fanshaw where they caught up with everything that had happened in one another lives since they'd been parted.

Grandmother spoke of some of the other patients on the ward. One or two had been dreadfully distressed and would take to the corridors weeping and wailing at night.

'That must have been difficult for you to sleep then?' Lucy said as she patted the woman's hand.

Lady Fanshaw nodded her head. 'Occasionally it was, but thankfully it didn't go on for too long when Nurse O' Connor was in charge. She's from Southern Ireland and has a lovely sing song voice. She could lull them to sleep with one of her songs from the old country.'

And I suspect a special pill or two, Lucy thought. It was good to see Grandmother back on form like this.

'What else did you do?' she wanted to know.

'Well, during the day following breakfast, there were various therapies and workshops as they called them for us to attend. I quite enjoyed those as they made the days pass a lot faster.'

'Oh?' Lucy arched an eyebrow.

'Things like basket making, weaving, embroidery, that sort of thing.'

Amused, Lucy sat forward in her chair having great difficulty imagining her grandmother weaving a basket or using needlepoint.

'But what I liked best of all…' she continued with a gleam in her eyes, 'was the painting. That was the most therapeutic of all, and is something I'd like to keep going as I get so much pleasure from creating something from nothing. I've left my artwork behind at the hospital as Nurse O'Connor said she'd like to frame the pieces for the other patients to enjoy.' A little smile crept onto Grandma's face.

'I had no idea you liked to paint…' Lucy said, quite awestruck by it all but then she remembered being told that her own mother had been artistic when she was young. Then something else struck her. 'That painting of Mama that hangs in the hall back at the big house, that was your work, wasn't it?'

Slowly, Grandmother nodded. 'Oh, painting was something I did as a young girl but when I married and wanted my own studio, your grandfather frowned on such frippery as he called it and forbade me from having one. Not so much as a paintbrush or a sketch book was allowed in the home.' She looked away and Lucy realised there was sadness in her heart about it. 'Apparently, it wasn't appropriate for someone of my social standing to be doing something like that. I'm sure he thought I was dancing with the fairies or something,' she smiled but her eyes were brimming with tears.

'But how did you come to paint my mother as a young woman then?' Lucy was puzzled.

'It was the only painting I painted after his death, just that one, then I laid down my brushes until this time.'

'I think it's wonderful you have so much talent, Grandma. I shall ask Sheldon if there are any shops that sell art supplies in the vicinity.'

Grandmother sniffed as if to hold back her tears. Lucy handed her a handkerchief and the woman dabbed at her eyes, then smiled as if she had a strange faraway wistful look on her face and she wondered what the woman was thinking of.

'A penny for them?' she asked.

'I was just remembering an old friend of mine called Joshua Blake…'

'Oh?'

'Joshua shared my passion for art as he was an artist himself.'

Lucy noticed a catch in her grandmother's voice. 'Really?'

'Yes, he was so good to me.' She swallowed hard. 'I'm afraid to admit that I let him down rather badly.'

Lucy reached out and touched the woman's hand. 'How was that?'

'Because I left him for your grandfather. You see, Joshua had proposed to me but I wanted to see more of life and the opportunities your grandfather offered me...' She looked into Lucy's eyes. Was her grandmother trying to tell her something about Archie, maybe? Was she comparing her granddaughter's relationships with Archie and Sheldon to herself with Joshua and the man she married? But how could she possibly have known Archie had proposed as the woman had been so drugged up by that nurse, she barely knew her own name at that time. Nevertheless, there was a lesson in there somewhere for her to learn.

Chapter Seventeen

1874

"The Hero"

The following day at school, far from getting a bruising from the older boys for attacking Ashcroft and knocking him to the ground, as he'd expected, instead Archie noticed some were smiling at him in acknowledgement or nodding their heads when previously they'd have ignored him, unless it was to run some errand for them or tell him off for running in the corridor. From his own peer group, he received pats on the back, comments of admiration and some even shared food items from their tucker with him.

'Don't you realise what you've done, Archie?' Carruthers asked.

He honestly didn't. 'Just had a bit of a spar with Ashcroft, that's all. I've been training for weeks.'

'No, no!' said the boy in excitement. 'It's much more than that, you've taken on the biggest bully in the school and won!'

A loud cheer went up as the boys threw their top hats up in the air. 'Long live, Archie! Long live the King!'

Archie found himself hoisted onto their shoulders as they carried him along, all the while chanting, their voices echoing off the corridor walls. Then he found himself carted outside through the main school entrance and bumping down the steps. Then the boys' voices suddenly fell silent and their mouths popped open in shock.

Ashcroft was going somewhere. Archie stared at the scene before him in disbelief. The boy was boarding a coach as his trunk was loaded on the top by the driver.

One of the older boys looked up at Archie as the boys still held him aloft on their shoulders, and smiled. 'Ashcroft is leaving us for good!'

'But why?' asked Archie.

The boy chuckled, 'He'd never be able to hold his head up again if he stayed, would he? He's picked on young lads for as long as I can remember, and now, for the first time one has fought back and floored him! And didn't he deserve it and all. Well done, young man! He'd forever be a figure of fun at this school! A six former being defeated by a first year! It's never been heard of before. You have one great right hook there, fella!' he said cheerfully. 'Next term, you'll be eligible to join the rugger and cricket teams, if someone puts a good word in for you.'

'Honestly?' Archie blinked in amazement.

'Yes. And not only that, next term they should make you head boy of your year. I'll be vouching for you as you've been looking out for others. An admirable quality indeed!'

Archie felt puffed up with pride at just how popular he was with both the younger pupils at the school and those in their senior years.

Archie's classmates lowered him down and he stood side by side with the senior pupil who said to him, 'Come along, young fellow, or we'll miss waving a fond farewell to old Ashcroft!' He chuckled as Ashcroft glowered at the pair of them through the cab window, his face red with embarrassment or was it fury? Archie wasn't quite sure, but it gave him a feeling of satisfaction that the school was finally rid of the bullying brute forever.

Then the horses sprang into action as the pair watched the coach veer its way down the long gravel drive until it reached the large wrought iron gates and departed for the long road outside.

The older boy patted Archie on his back. 'I'm Cudmore, by the way. Thomas Cudmore but you can call me Tom any time,' the lad said good naturedly.

'I'm Archie.'

'I know,' said Tom. 'The whole school is talking about you. No one will mess you around anymore, believe me.'

Archie smiled as he followed the lad back in through the school entrance as his classmates looked on in absolute awe.

***

Over the years, Archie became the most popular boy at the school, representing it in all the popular sports of the day including rugby, cricket, and of course, boxing. By the time he entered the sixth form, he was voted in by everyone there as head boy of the entire school. Never again under his watch would a young boy, or older boy for that matter, have to worry about being bullied. He employed a team of boys to watch out for everyone, so the boys themselves could go to him in confidence if need be to report an incident, so that it was nipped in the bud. There was to be no tolerance whatsoever towards bullying at the school and even the headmaster and masters were now on board with this principle.

By the time Archie left Compton Manor School he was quite the young man and ready to face the world.

Chapter Eighteen

1885

"The Woman in Black"

Lucy and Sheldon were out for a stroll in the park in the warm afternoon sunshine when, taking her hand, he turned to her and said, 'You know I'll miss you when you return to England, don't you?'

She nodded shyly because she had half expected this moment, the moment when things would change and never, ever be the same again.

His breaths became ragged and she could see the depth of feeling he had for her reflected in his charcoal eyes as they softened and settled on her own. In that moment, she could sense that swell of love for her more acutely than at any other time. The leaves on the trees rustled around them and the autumnal wind blew hard, sending some leaves twirling and finally scattering on the ground at their feet as a carpet containing the hues of russet, orange and gold.

By the time these trees were bare, she'd be back on the steamer ship sailing for home. But now…this.

'Lucy,' he said, almost nervously. 'I've known you long enough. Long enough to realise how much I want you in my life. I can't bear the thought of never seeing you again. Of never having you in my life.'

He knelt down and taking a box from his pocket, produced the most beautiful emerald and diamond ring she'd ever seen in her life as it sparkled and shone in the many facets from the sun during a crisp autumnal afternoon.

Breathlessly, she gasped, as both her hands flew to her face in surprise.

'Would you do me the honour of being my wife?' He asked in earnest.

Although she had half expected him to say something as their time together was drawing to a close, she hadn't expected this. What could she say? Undoubtedly, she'd miss him too. But her heart remained with another who was a long way away on the other side of the Atlantic Ocean, someone who had also proposed.

But, nudged a little voice inside her, *Didn't that one forget you all so easily when things didn't go his way?*

'I really don't know what to say,' she said softly looking into his eyes. She so didn't want to disappoint him and felt she owed him a great debt of gratitude for all he'd done for her grandmother.

'Just say "yes" and I will be the happiest man in the whole wide world,' he replied.

She smiled down on him. 'Please give me adequate time to consider your proposal. This has come so out of the blue, Sheldon,' she said softly as her eyes began to mist with tears. Were they tears of happiness or the sadness she still felt inside her heart? She wasn't quite sure. It felt to her like a jigsaw puzzle with a missing piece she couldn't quite locate. But this man before her had a lot to offer.

'Of course, you must have time to consider carefully, honey,' he said quickly as he rose to his feet as if he feared rejection there and then. 'There's no question of that. I sprang my proposal on you out of the blue because I thought you'd return home without you ever knowing just how I feel about you.'

She nodded. 'I do understand.'

His eyes clouded over for a moment. 'No, I don't think you do, Lucy.' He paused for a moment. 'If you return to England, we might never see one another again.'

'Oh, I'm sure we would,' she said rather too glibly.

'No, we might not. Mother isn't getting any younger, and between you and I...' he glanced around as if fearful of being overheard, yet there was no one around, only a black cat sat upon the fence of the large house opposite, licking its paws.

'What is it?' she asked gently.

'It's her heart. It's not as strong as it was. She's always had somewhat of a delicate constitution but lately she's been having some sort of fainting spells and seems weakened by them afterwards. I got her checked out by a specialist at the hospital who has prescribed medication, but he says the condition will worsen over time...'

'Oh,' said Lucy. She hadn't been expecting to hear that and had become dreadfully fond of the woman. She'd hate to see anything happen to her.

'So, you see, I couldn't possibly make another trip overseas not right now. I'd promised her that the last one would be final for me as I want to take care of her.'

'But isn't there something they can do? Anything?'

He shook his head sadly.

'I'm afraid not.'

But she looks so fit and well for a woman of her age.'

'I know. That's another reason why I wanted to propose to you right now, so we can be married here and you can make Auburn your home.'

'But Grandma? What about her?'

'I'm sure when the time comes, Nurse Carmichael and the maid are more than capable of escorting your grandmother back home. Look, although I can't leave Mother, you would be free to visit your family in the future.'

She nodded. That was a possibility if she accepted his proposal that was.

'I'll give you plenty of time to think about things,' he said taking her by the arm. 'Meanwhile, there's a rather lovely tea shop around the corner I want to take you to. They make delicious sponge cakes loaded with whipped cream and strawberry jelly or jam as you charming British folk like to call it. So delicious.'

She nodded and smiled, although her stomach fluttered with anxiety. There were so many questions flooding her mind that she failed to see the determined lady who was following in their footsteps.

***

The tea room was located around the corner of the street so that it occupied property along the curve of two separate adjoining streets. It looked quite charming with its myriad of small window panes which created a bay effect along with the lace drapes adorning them. Lucy glanced up at the sign which read in gold lettering against a black background, *The Rosie Lea*. The name Rosie Lea was a comfort to her in a way as it was Cockney rhyming slang for a cup of tea and she wondered if there was some sort of connection with back home. A little bell tinkled overhead as they entered the establishment, which brought a stout middle-aged woman who wore a long black dress and white frilled pinafore, scurrying towards them with her hands clasped together as if in delight at seeing them both.

'Oh, my word,' she said, using a long Southern drawl which defined her as not being originally from the New York area. 'Ain't you the pretty one, ma'am.'

'Mrs Peterson, this is Miss Lucy Fanshaw from England.' Sheldon proudly introduced.

Immediately the woman was gushing, her eyes enlarged and Lucy thought she'd faint from the excitement of it all. 'England? Oh, my goodness. It's so great to see a customer here from all that way across the ocean. I've heard about the quaint castles you have over there and your lovely queen of course.'

Lucy stifled a giggle as the woman fawned on and on about England. As she glanced around the tea room it became apparent that the proprietor had modelled her shop on an English tea room as several paintings depicted. There was the Tower of London and Buckingham Palace and some which Lucy couldn't tell if they were in England or not but she guessed the green fields made them appear so, even if they weren't. Feeling slightly guilty for inwardly mocking the woman, she smiled and said, 'Thank you, Mrs Peterson. This is such a charming tea room you have here.'

The woman beamed and then led them to a little table near the window so they could see the world pass by outside. 'I'll send my best waitress, Amelia, over shortly to take your order. Meanwhile, please peruse our afternoon tea menu.'

Was that a posh English accent Mrs Peterson put on there for a moment? Lucy wasn't sure. She'd once met an Australian gentleman at The Horse and Harness back in Whitechapel—the woman's put-on accent sounded very similar to that, sort of English but with an unusual sort of twang.

Sheldon drew out a chair for Lucy to seat her at the table then he followed suit himself opposite. He removed his leather gloves laying them down neatly on the table and lifted the menu to peruse it, then glanced at Lucy over the top of it with smiling eyes. He whispered, 'Isn't she simply terrible?'

Which caused Lucy to giggle. 'Yes.'

'She's always like that but more so if she wants to impress. You really must tell her some cock and bull story about your Queen of England, she'll be living off it for months.'

Lucy felt her face flush. 'Oh, I couldn't do that to the lady.'

'If you don't, I shall,' he said, then he set down the menu and twirled his moustache in merriment.

She hadn't seen this side of him before, the mischievous side, it was almost as though he were a young boy again.

The doorbell tinkled and immediately Lucy noticed that Sheldon paled significantly as someone entered the establishment. His features appeared set in stone, almost statue-like. 'What's the matter?' she asked. 'You've gone as white as a ghost.'

'Er, nothing,' he muttered, then taking a large white cotton handkerchief from his jacket pocket, he blotted his forehead.

She swallowed hard. Something or someone was troubling him, that much was evident and she guessed that someone was the person who had just entered the tea room but unfortunately, as she was seated with her back towards the door, she couldn't see who it was who had entered. Thinking on her feet, she said to a passing waitress, 'Excuse me, miss. Would you happen to have a ladies' convenience here?'

'Sure, ma'am,' the young girl said, 'it's just over there…' she pointed.

Lucy thanked her and excused herself from the table. There had been few customers when they arrived, so she scanned the room to see who it might be and then she saw her in the corner. A young woman, who was probably a few years older than herself, seated there as if pretending to be unaware of her surroundings as she perused the menu. Her blonde hair was scooped up in an elegant chignon beneath her dark veiled hat. The rest of her clothing was dark too which made Lucy wonder if the woman was in mourning. She glanced at Lucy as she passed by and for some reason, she felt her cheeks burn. What was it about the woman? Her emerald green eyes caught Lucy's and seemed to bore a hole inside her. Who was she to Sheldon?

She took her time in the ladies' room to compose herself. She didn't really need the lavatory so she used the jug of water to splash over her face and she dried it in one of the folded small pristine white towels that lay by the side of the washbasin and jug. No way did she want to return in there looking hot and flustered. She decided to sneak a peek by the door as she opened it slightly to see what was going on inside the tea room. Sheldon, it seemed to her, was purposely staring out of the window to avoid the woman's gaze. But from where she was stood behind a wooden lattice screen that divided the tea room in two halves, she couldn't see the woman. She decided to wait a little longer to see what he'd do, but then she noticed the woman must have got up from the table as she was standing in front of a worried looking Sheldon who was saying something to her and patting his forehead with his handkerchief again. She watched as he ran a finger beneath the collar of his shirt as if it was suddenly too tight for him. The woman, whoever she was, was making him feel highly uncomfortable, that much was evident. Lucy's heart began to beat faster as he stood and appeared to be escorting the woman out of the establishment. She waited a little longer until he returned to the tearoom and took his seat. Should she tell him what she'd just witnessed, or say nothing?

As she approached the table, he stood as a mark of respect, which she noted he hadn't done when the lady in black had approached. Where was she now, anyhow? Was she still waiting outside?

'H…have you decided what you'd like?' he asked as he pulled her chair out and waited for her to seat herself.

'Oh, there's so much choice, I really don't know,' she said, her mind no longer on eating.

'Then I'll choose for us,' he said as he reseated himself. It was as if he was almost forcing himself to think of something else, anything other than that woman. He quickly scanned the menu then announced, 'How about a plate of cucumber sandwiches and the English scones with jam and clotted cream? Oh, and a pot of your

English tea, too,' he added, snapping shut the menu, then laying it down on the table. His voice sounded overly bright to her as if he was forcing himself to appear in a happy mood, which disturbed her greatly.

The waitress had noticed him laying down the menu as if ready to be served, so she arrived at the table to take their order. When she'd departed, before she even thought about it, Lucy asked, 'Sheldon, who was that lady in black who spoke to you just now?'

'You saw?' he asked, his eyes widening and almost unblinking for a few seconds.

'Yes,' she nodded and waited for him to answer.

His face reddened. 'I didn't want to tell you this but she was an old flame of mine...'

'Really?' Why didn't she believe him?

'Yes. It's always awkward if we bump into one another as I'm afraid I let her down really badly.'

'Did you?'

'Yes, we were engaged for a time but then I had my career and you know how life is.'

Lucy furrowed her brow. The lady looked a lot older than Sheldon, it didn't make sense to her. 'So, why was she dressed in black?'

'Oh, that's easy to answer,' he said, as if almost relieved. 'Her husband passed away a few months ago.'

'Did you know him?'

'Er, no...' He looked up as the waitress arrived at the table and laid down a double tiered cake stand which contained miniature sandwiches at the top and the scones on the bottom plate. Lucy got the distinct impression Sheldon was relieved that the conversation was interrupted and that concerned her. No more was said about the matter as they ate, and as they walked back to the house, a little voice inside warned, *Do you really know this man at all?* But she chose to ignore it.

Chapter Nineteen

1885

"A Funeral to Attend"

Archie stood gazing out of the window. It was now a few months since he'd had the riding accident and little pieces of his memory were slowly coming back to him. There were small fragments that returned clearly, like the coach falling into trouble and taking the horse off at speed and toppling off it and hitting his head. Then there was a memory of waking up in that strange coaching house but he couldn't for the life of him remember why he'd been in such a hurry that day. The same thing had happened to dear Uncle Walter when he'd slipped and hit his head on a rock when out fishing years ago. He recalled that eventually things came back to him, but it took time. Archie's head injury was nowhere near as bad as his uncle's though. He'd been saved by missing those cobblestones and ending up on the dirt track road instead. He needed now to fit the small fragments of memory together to make sense of it all.

There was a light knock on the door. 'Sir?'

He glanced across the room to see Baxter stood there with a silver tray in his hand which appeared to contain some sort of letter. The old man's hand was trembling slightly which Archie put down to his age. Now Baxter was someone he did remember very clearly.

'I thought you should see this, Sir,' he said. 'A young boy delivered it and said it's important that you read it right away.'

Feeling concerned and with butterflies in his stomach, he walked towards the man and took the letter from the tray, then opened it with the letter knife provided which he dropped back on the tray with a clatter.

His heart sank as he digested the words.

The funeral of Nathaniel Knight will take place on October the ninth at St Michael's Church in Crownley at 10 o'clock. Refreshments will be taken afterwards at Meadowcroft Manor.

Archie let out a little gasp.

'What is it, Sir?'

'It…it's Nathaniel Knight. He's p…passed away,' he said in disbelief as he shook his head.

'I'm sorry to hear that. He was a lovely gentleman.'

'Yes, he was.' Archie found it strange thinking about the man in the past tense. Another thought occurred to him, how would Lucy be informed of this? The man was after all, her step father, and now she was somewhere across the Continent, he believed. He had a vague memory of her telling him she was leaving and he knew he would miss her but he had honestly thought she'd be back by now.

As if sensing something was up, Baxter looked at him and asked, 'What's troubling you, Sir?'

'It's Lucy. I was just thinking that she'll have to return for the funeral.'

'I don't think that's possible, Sir. Not when she's so far away.'

'But France, where I believe she went, isn't that far away, she could be home in a couple of days in time for it if someone got a telegram to her, surely?'

Baxter shook his head in disbelief. 'Your uncle informed you after your accident that she'd gone to America.'

'America! I just don't understand...' then it came back at him. He'd been speaking to her just days before she was leaving for the trip with her grandmother. There'd been something he'd asked her and he'd been in a rush to see her off.

'Yes, apparently she didn't realise herself she was going there, she was under the illusion it was to France but her grandmother had other ideas. You know how strong-willed Lady Fanshaw is.'

'Absolutely, but America.' It was only the thought of seeing Lucy again soon that had kept him going. No wonder he hadn't received any letters from her and she must have wondered why he hadn't shown up to see her off.

Sadly, he glanced at the letter once more and laid it back on the tray. Then in a stoic voice said, 'If you can place that letter in the top drawer of my desk, please. I shall attend of course. And if you can get my black suit ready along with a white shirt by Friday for me, I shall be most grateful.' He paused for a moment. 'Baxter?'

'Sir?'

'Any idea what Mr Knight died of? He always seemed so fit and healthy to me?'

Baxter shook his head. 'No, Sir. But if I hear anything from the other servants, I'll let you know.'

Archie nodded gratefully as he watched the elderly man turn to leave the room. If anyone knew it would be one of the servants as they were always out and about in the village and gossip raged like wild fire there.

The morning was bitterly cold as Archie set off for the funeral. He wrapped his muffler tightly around his neck and turned up the collar on his astrakhan coat.

'Are you sure you won't take the carriage, Sir?' Baxter called after him. But Archie didn't even turn around to look at the man, preferring instead to gesticulate "farewell" with the back of his hand. The truth was, he had butterflies in the pit of his stomach at the thought of the funeral and his connection to Lucy. It was unlikely she'd be there of course but at least he might get to speak to someone who'd be in the know about when she might return home. But that wasn't the real reason he was choosing to attend, he'd genuinely liked and respected Nathaniel Knight, who'd been a true gentleman indeed. A fine upstanding man who had helped the villagers of Crownley. He'd amassed several properties in recent years which had been bequeathed to him in his grandfather's will. He'd rented them out to folk at reasonable prices. For those who had fallen on hard times, instead of ejecting them from their homes when they couldn't pay like the previous squire, he'd allowed them to carry on. Even supplying a roof over their heads, allowing them to pay what they could until they got back on their feet. He'd been a firm but fair landlord. And if they couldn't pay anything at all, he'd given them work on his estate. Adella had been kind too, checking on the welfare of tenants and had once ended up nursing the mother of one family back to good health. Whilst the woman was ill, she had taken it upon herself to roll up the sleeves of her dress and she'd selflessly fed and watered the family as well as cleaning their house from top to bottom. It was amazing, Archie thought. Although both Adella and Nathaniel had come from great wealth, they hadn't been afraid to get their hands dirty at all.

He wondered for a moment how Lady Fanshaw was doing and if Lucy was still her companion for the duration of their trip? The last he'd heard was the woman only had months left to live. How dreadful it would be for Lucy when that happened, the pair had become so close.

Whenever he thought of Lucy, her smile and her glittering brown eyes came to his mind. But try as he might, right now he just couldn't picture her face as a grown woman only as the young kitchen maid back at the coaching inn at Whitechapel. He guessed he'd fallen in love with her right then and there as she'd stood on that old wooden crate to reach the sink to wash the dishes. Somehow, he could visualise her as an adult and a lady in a beautiful satin gown with her dark brown hair lying in ringlets on her shoulders, it was her face he failed to picture. The child Lucy he could bring to mind quite easily but not the adult.

Small white snowflakes had begun to fall as Archie left the drive way and exited via the large double wrought iron gates towards the main road outside. He looked heavenward at the leaden sky and wondered what Lucy was doing right now? Was she missing him as much as he was missing her? Or had she forgotten all about him as she lived the high life with Lady Fanshaw? He pulled himself up sharp as he remembered the elderly lady was dying. This was intended as one last trip. Of course, she wouldn't be enjoying herself when she had so many concerns. Not least of all what she would do without her beloved grandmother when she was no longer around.

He walked for some time until he saw the village in the distance with its thatched roofs and curling smoke emanating from many chimneys. Even the village pond was iced over and a small crowd of children had gathered to play. A sign had been recently installed warning of the dangers of thin ice and he realised that either Nathaniel or Adella would have ensured that. What could have possibly happened in such a short space of time to cause his death? Baxter had asked the staff as he'd suggested, but none of them really knew anything. It was a mystery.

Snowflakes had begun to settle on his top hat and the shoulders of his black coat but thankfully, it was only a slight dusting. There would be more to come later though, he was sure of it.

The church spire stood out loud and proud in the distance surrounded by skeletal trees with sparse leaves, and he made his way solemnly there. As he did so, he shivered as a pair of black regal looking horses wearing black plumage and blinkers, rode past pulling a carriage with two top hatted gentleman seated on top, which he figured were the undertakers as behind them in the glass fronted carriage, was the oak wood coffin of Nathaniel Knight, squire of the village. It was adorned with pristine white lilies and green trailing ivy foliage.

From inside the church he heard the sounds of the piped organ playing a song he vaguely recognised from childhood. *Jesu Joy of Man's Desiring* began drifting towards him and it brought back a strong and vivid memory of when he and his mother attended church on a Sunday. The congregation was always gregarious at that particular church as the people of the East End tended to be friendly and welcoming as a whole. Especially his next-door neighbour, Ginny, who had been like another mother to him.

He watched as an elderly lady and gentleman, in black attire, entered the church and he followed suit behind them. He was just in time as the vicar stood in the vestibule ready to welcome the hearse.

After being greeted by the man with a firm handshake and a few words of condolence, Archie made his way into the main part of the building and found an empty pew at the back of the church. His eyes scanned the nave towards the altar for any sign of Adella. There were too many heads for him to see past so he guessed that he would have to wait until the service was over or he'd attend back at the house later.

The only clue to what might have happened to cause Mr Knight's death was when the reverend mentioned an illness that had swept over the man and taken hold like a thief in the night claiming his life. What that illness was he could only imagine but whatever it had been was swift and deadly.

There were several bible readings and hymns and then a man, he did not recognise, stepped up to the green velvet covered podium to speak about the life of Nathaniel Knight, how he had been a benevolent sort thinking only of others. Archie knew this to be true as Lucy was a testament to that, the man had been instrumental in saving her mother and getting them together in the end. Oh, how her heart must be breaking as Mrs Adella Knight, the lady of the manor, she would be so bereft to now go it alone. The man then went on to explain that Mr Knight had died from pneumonia. He had dived into the river on his own property to rescue a drowning lad who had been fishing there, and although he'd saved the life of the boy, he'd lost his own when several days later his cold had turned to pneumonia which had ravaged his lungs and cost him his life.

Poor Nathaniel. Now Archie knew at last what had killed the man. His kindness and bravery had robbed him of his life. Probably the lad had been fishing there illegally too, but that wouldn't have mattered to him as he looked after the villagers' welfare—a young boy's safety would have held more importance to him than a spot of illegal fishing.

Why was life so unkind? The ten years of happiness Adella had since known with Nathaniel had cruelly been snatched away from her. Although no longer young, she wasn't old either. He guessed she was in her mid thirties maybe? Not too old to begin again but where would someone of Adella's standing find a new husband? Prospective suitors might be after her money and her upcoming inheritance when her mother passed away, which might not be much longer by the sound of it.

A surge of guilt flooded through him as he realised in his mind he was already planning Adella's future life with a new husband onboard when this one wasn't even cold in his coffin yet, nor had he even been laid to rest.

The reverend then spoke of Mr Knight as having lived a deep and meaningful life as both a Christian and a philanthropist. Then he recited Psalm twenty-three, *The Lord is My Shepherd*, which he invited the congregation to join in with.

Yea though I walk through the valley of the shadow of death, I will fear no evil: for thou art with me...

As the congregation collectively recited the words, a shiver ran down Archie's spine.

It was then he heard a female voice weep loudly and unashamedly from the front pew of the church and he realised it was Adella, it was almost guttural somehow. Her pain reverberated deeply with him as he remembered his own heart wrenching feeling of loss as a young boy at his mother's funeral service. Ginny had led him through the graveyard and laid a reassuring hand on his shoulder as his mother had been laid to rest. Not even his loving and kind friend and neighbour, dear loyal Ginny, could absolve the grief he'd felt that welled up inside him like a bottomless pit of despair. It was many years before he felt, not healed, he could never say that, but comforted and almost whole, though there would always be a part of him missing, he knew that.

The sobs were getting louder as they seemed to echo around the church walls and in a fit of intuition as to how the woman was feeling, he rose from his pew and rushed to the front where he took her hand and laid a comforting hand on her shoulder as he sat beside her. Where was everyone? Her family? She was in the front pew totally alone. He could see the servants seated respectfully in the pew behind, but they looked confused as if unsure what to do next. He turned and nodded to them and just held Adella's hand as everyone left the church and she cried like a child, then he held her in his arms as her shoulders wracked with the overwhelming grief she felt at losing the only man she had ever loved.

Chapter Twenty

1885

"A Change of Behaviour"

Lucy had noticed how oddly Sheldon was behaving for several days in a row. He became quiet and uncommunicative as if mulling things over in his mind. She became so concerned about him that she asked his mother one afternoon.

'There's no need for you to worry,' his mother said softly, 'he's prone to fits of melancholia from time to time.'

'But I've never seen him like this before,' Lucy protested.

The woman smiled and laid a reassuring hand on Lucy's shoulder. 'Believe me, I've seen him like this more times than I care to remember since his father's death...he'll be all right in the end.'

Regardless of what Sheldon's mother said, though, Lucy had the instinct that something wasn't right at all and maybe she should speak to him about whatever was troubling him.

Breaking into her thoughts, Violet said, 'I think it would be nice if we took tea in the conservatory this afternoon, would your grandmother like to join us?'

Lucy beamed. 'Yes, that would be lovely, I'll just go to her room to check on her.'

Violet nodded and Lucy left to climb the stairs to her grandmother's bedroom. Once outside the bedroom door, she knocked gently to hear the woman say, 'Enter,' in a soft voice.

She popped her head through the partially open door. 'Violet has asked us to join her later for tea in the conservatory, Grandma. How would you like that?'

Lady Fanshaw nodded and smiled, 'Yes, I'd like that but there's something I must speak to you about first.' Was she imagining things or was her grandmother frowning there? It was almost as if her smile was pasted on her face which was most unusual as usually Grandma was an open book. She didn't mind telling people exactly what she thought.

'Oh?' Lucy quirked an inquisitive brow.

Grandma patted the bed for Lucy to sit down whilst she took a seat in the wicker chair beside it.

What had grandma in mind? Did she feel ill again?

She hesitated before speaking as she looked up at the ceiling as if choosing her words carefully. Then she looked directly into Lucy's eyes. 'I'm sorry to tell you, that it's time for us to return home...'

Lucy's heart plummeted. 'But I thought the plan was to stay here another month or so and return in time for Christmas?'

'It's not that, I'd love to stay myself but I'm sorry to have to say this but I've received word that Nathaniel has passed away rather suddenly and your mother needs us both. A telegram arrived earlier when you were out strolling in the grounds. I'm sorry but it's taken me this long to compose myself before I could bring myself to tell you. You know how fond I was of Nathaniel. I can't help thinking about your poor mother…'

Suddenly, Lucy burst into tears. The shock of hearing the news was making her feel dizzy, the room was spinning and she heard her grandmother cry out. The next thing she knew she was lying on the bed with Sheldon looking down at her, as he knelt at her side, gently smoothing her forehead.

***

'What happened?' he asked as Grandma looked on with deep concern etched on her features.

'It's my fault, I'm afraid,' she let out a long breath before continuing, 'I should have chosen my words more carefully but I didn't know how to tell her any other way that Nathaniel has passed away.'

Sheldon shook his head. 'No, you mustn't worry about that, how else were you meant to deliver bad news? She'll be fine. I'll get someone to bring her a cold glass of water. She'll be right as rain in no time,' he said in a reassuring tone of voice. Then to Lucy, 'You cry it out, honey. It really is the best thing when you lose someone you love. Believe me, I should know.' He took hold of her hand as she wept profusely, feeling comforted by his touch.

Grandma was already hovering by the door with her hand on the doorknob, 'I'll summon the maid for that glass of water now,' she said firmly, sounding much more like the strong woman she had been before she'd taken the laudanum.

'Now then young lady, I thought this Nathaniel was an old beau of yours for you to have acted so strongly?' he said with a twinkle in his eyes as she looked up at him.

'Oh no, no, he was more like a father to me. He married my mother, so he's my stepfather you see. Grandmother plans for us to leave as soon as possible to spend time with my mother...'

She noticed his eyes darkening momentarily. 'Then if you leave, please allow me to come with you,' his lips claimed hers before she knew it and she melted in his arms. How could she bear to be parted from him?

She gently pulled away as a thought occurred to her. 'But what about your mother, I thought you said you can't possibly leave her as she's too unwell?'

'I daresay she'll understand if I tell her we are to marry as soon as possible and that England will be our honeymoon, then we'll return and make our home here. I'll never have to leave her again.' He looked at her in expectation and she felt he was using this as an opportunity to push ahead with marriage plans when she hadn't even said "Yes" as yet.

She smiled, it should have been all that she wanted to hear that they were to be married soon, but there was a still small voice which reminded her that things were going far too fast.

Chapter Twenty-One
1885
"December"

Archie was looking forward to Christmas this year. His beloved Lucy was returning from New York. Apparently, according to Adella, she had been staying at a doctor's home in Auburn. He found that most strange as surely if an overseas trip had been arranged, they would all be staying in a hotel? How had she encountered the man? Anyhow, from what Adella had told him on the afternoon of her husband's funeral, word had been sent that Lucy and Lady Fanshaw were on their way home and would arrive well in time for the festive season. He couldn't imagine there'd be much festivity taking place though as it would all happen under a shadow of grief, which was a shame as Adella had told him that apparently her mother was now in good health once again. That had seemed so odd to him too as the last time he'd seen her she did look poorly indeed, but Adella had explained how Lucy had written to inform her that Nurse Carmichael had been overdosing her mother on doctor's orders with laudanum. No wonder the poor lady had been so querulous some of the time when he'd visited Lucy. Other times, she'd barely been able to hold a conversation with her nearest and dearest.

If Lucy had taken the time to write to her mother why couldn't she have written to him? That truly stung. Still, she was due home and he was so looking forward to it. The engagement ring he'd presented her with before she'd left was safely locked away in his desk drawer and he planned to offer it to her again on Christmas Eve.

'You're spirited today, sir?' Baxter said quite suddenly, taking Archie by surprise, he hadn't even heard his approach.

He turned to face the man and nodded. 'I am indeed, Baxter. Lucy and her grandmother will be home before Christmas.'

'Splendid, sir!' Baxter said with a big smile on his face. 'Are you planning to do anything special?'

'Well for a start, I must see my tailor in Savile Row as I need some new shirts and I quite fancy a smartly tailored jacket and a gold brocade waistcoat, maybe some new cravats too.'

Baxter nodded approvingly. 'Sounds as though you're out to impress, sir?'

Archie smiled. He found any mention of Lucy was enough to paste a soppy smile on his face these days. 'Maybe I am. I feel so wretched about letting her down the time she left England.'

'But that was hardly your fault, sir. You had an accident and lost your memory for some time.'

And didn't he feel guilty about that and all. He shouldn't have, everyone told him so, but it was only recently his memory had returned and he'd explained it all now to Adella who said that she thought Lucy would be pleased to see him again.

'I suppose if I had been in my right mind and remembered in time, I could have asked Mrs Knight for her daughter's contact address and then I could have written to Lucy. I do hope she'll forgive me.'

'I'm sure she already has, sir. Now I believe that Cook is about to dish up dinner a little earlier this evening?'

'Yes,' he brightened. 'I've asked her to as I have someone important calling to the house, very important indeed.'

Baxter quirked an enquiring brow but didn't ask him any questions. The important person calling to the house was the reverend from the local church. Archie was hoping to propose over Christmas and arrange a New Year's Day wedding should Lucy agree. Surely she would agree as she'd be stopping home for good now her grandmother was well again.

***

Standing at the bottom of the drive of the Knightly residence, Archie blew on his gloveless hands. He could have reprimanded himself for leaving them behind on the hall table at home when he'd removed them last moment to sign something. For it was not proper etiquette for a gentleman to arrive without his gloves in situ or without a hat, either, thankfully he had remembered that. Yet, how many times on the streets of Whitechapel had he gone without any gloves at all, even in harsh weather? But there'd been little choice when he'd been at the hands of Bill Brackley. Sometimes he'd even ended up barefoot, particularly when he climbed those searing chimney breasts; but all of that was a world away and now today as he stood there with his heart atremble at the thought of encountering Lucy, he smiled to himself. It would be so good to see her once again, but what he asked himself was, would she be pleased to see him? He was about to find out.

He dismissed his carriage driver who drove it around to the rear of the property. It was normal practice for drivers to find a welcome and some refreshment in the friendly, warm kitchen of large houses. A steaming cup of tea and maybe a slice of fruit cake or some other delicious concoction was most welcome on a cold winter's day. Come to that, depending on the cook's benevolence other tradesmen and women often found solace there too. He remembered that well enough from his time delivering pies for Bessie Harper and that's how he'd met Mr Baxter his butler of course.

He let out a long breath into the frosty early afternoon air as he approached the walnut coloured front door with its holly wreath decorated with pine cones and red and green ribbon, displaying to all that the festive season was upon them, even if the inhabitants of the house were plagued with grief.

A maid answered the door and she directed him to the drawing room where he was welcomed by Adella. She approached him with outstretched hands which he took into his own. He looked into her watery eyes to see the sadness within, but the woman was obviously trying her best to maintain an air of dignity and attempting to keep cheerful, despite the circumstances. He had to admire her for that.

'My, but you're perished,' she said, taking a long look at him.

'Please excuse me. I forgot my gloves,' he admitted, and then felt his face flush with embarrassment like when he'd been a young boy and had done something that turned all eyes towards him. Like the time Old Penny at Compton Manor School had unintentionally humiliated him about his real father in front of his class mates. But it wasn't so much that he'd usually get embarrassed by something so trivial as a missing pair of gloves, it was more to do with the fact he was about to encounter the love of his life once again. How Lucy would have such stories to tell him. He didn't really know anyone who'd been to America but his uncle had always said he'd take him some day, but he was so absorbed in his new wife he could never imagine that day ever happening.

'Is Lucy here, yet?' he asked expectantly. He couldn't wait to ask the question that had been poised on his lips since he'd first arrived.

Adella's eyes widened, then she lowered her voice a notch. 'Archie, there's something I need to tell you…'

The door opened suddenly behind them and there she was, her dark curls cascading on her shoulders, her brown eyes sparking. She was wearing the most fashionable looking teal green silk gown he'd ever seen with puffed sleeves, a nipped in waist and a sweetheart neckline. Lucy was framed in the doorway like the subject of an Old Masters painting—his heart melted for her.

There was something about her though. What was it? She seemed more of a woman somehow as if in those months across the Atlantic Ocean she had suddenly matured. The swell of her breasts beneath her bodice, the faint rose hue to her cheeks. It was as if she'd left the shores of England as a young lady and returned as a woman.

'L…Lucy,' he stammered as he walked towards.

'Archie!' she said excitedly and he could tell she was pleased to see him. He had no more fears, all would be well. 'It's lovely to see you after all this time.'

Adella exchanged glances with Lucy. 'You'll have to tell him,' she said to her daughter.

'Tell me what?' Were they about to play some kind of practical joke on him? He wasn't sure. He smiled nervously, unaware what was to happen next.

'Listen, Archie,' Lucy said, as she slowly walked towards him. 'There's something I need to tell you…'

'Yes?' he blinked several times.

'I'm now a…'

'A what?'

'A married woman,' said a male voice from behind her in an accent he couldn't quite place. Who was the dashing looking fellow now stood at Lucy's side, gazing adoringly at her? This really had to be some kind of joke, hadn't it?

'It's true,' said Lucy, as the gentleman beside her took her hand in his. 'This is my new husband, Sheldon. Doctor Sheldon Harrington,' she said proudly. 'He's also an author who uses the pen name Sheldon Harper Brown…'

Suddenly, he felt the room spinning. This had to be a bad dream.

As if sensing what was about to happen, Adella turned to the small occasional table behind her and poured Archie a small glass of brandy from a crystal decanter. 'I think we'll take a glass for Christmas,' she said, pasting a smile on her face. She hurriedly handed a glass to Archie which he accepted gratefully and then one to Sheldon, while for herself and Lucy she poured a schooner of sherry each. How clever of the woman to realise how distressed he felt and turning it into a celebration instead and for that he was extremely grateful. He took a moment to collect his thoughts as the amber fluid warmed him and a thousand questions flitted through his mind. Lucy married? To this man stood in front of him and who was a doctor? Not only that but he was some sort of author too? And from New York, no less.

None of it made any sense to him, most of his memory had been restored but a piece of the jigsaw was missing for him. The little piece that left a gap which made him wonder what it was that was absent here? Could Lucy have possibly known this Sheldon before she went away and that was why she'd turned down his proposal in the first place? And to save face, she'd allowed him to think it was really because she was going away with her dying grandmother? Surely not?

'To friends and family!' Adella said, raising her glass which caused everyone to mirror her actions.

'To friends and family!' Sheldon said as he eyed Archie in a curious fashion. Maybe the man was just as astonished as he was.

The only person Archie could think of who could shine any light on this for him as she had been there herself was Lady Fanshaw?

He nodded at Adella. 'To us all!' he said and then pausing to swallow a lump that had formed in his throat, asked, 'but where is Lady Fanshaw this afternoon?'

Adella smiled. 'Mother will be along with us shortly. She's been resting but when I told her you were due, she said she couldn't wait to see you. She's always been fond of you, Archie.'

Sheldon quirked a brow. 'Archie? Is that your real name or some sort of nick name?'

Archie gritted his teeth? Who did this man think he was? 'My full name is Archibald but everyone calls me Archie and has done so since I was a young boy.'

Sheldon cleared his throat as if he didn't quite believe what he was hearing. 'And what do you do for a living…er…Archie?'

'I'm a landowner,' Archie said firmly. 'I own my own estate now and the land to go with it.'

'An inheritance I presume?'

'You presume correctly, yes.'

This man was beginning to infuriate him. Was it because he was now married to Lucy and had taken the only woman he'd ever truly loved or was it something else? But from the impudence of the fellow, Archie decided that Lucy aside, the man would have got his goat anyhow. He had an air of arrogance about him that Archie didn't much care for and there was something else too…he aroused Archie's suspicions for some reason. He had no idea why that would be, but there was something he didn't quite trust about him.

'We'll be dining in an hour or so but I suggest we all go for a little stroll in the grounds to increase our appetites,' Adella advised. 'Sheldon, I should like to speak to you and maybe Lucy, you could show Archie the new ornamental fountain and garden I've had installed to honour Nathaniel's memory?'

Lucy nodded. At last, it would be time to get Lucy on her own. Then he could ask her the questions that needed answering.

***

As they headed towards the fountain and gardens things felt awkward for a moment. They both kept their distance from one another, when normally they'd have linked arms and engaged in small talk. Then Archie spotted a wooden bench. 'Let's sit here for a moment,' he suggested.

Lucy nodded, almost shyly, reminding him of her the first time he'd encountered her. They both took a seat and then he turned to her and asked, 'What happened? I don't understand? One moment you were going to the Continent to be with your grandmother in her final days so you turned down my proposal of marriage, then the next thing I find out you didn't even go there. You went to New York instead, your grandmother is now well (which I'm glad about by the way, though rather puzzled), and now you return married to someone else?'

Lucy's face flushed and for a moment she couldn't meet his eyes but when she did, he could see the pain behind them. 'Oh, Archie, what did you expect me to think? You never even turned up to see me off. I waited, gazing over the side of the ship for as long as I possibly could. I had the faint hope in my heart that you were a little late and I'd catch you running alongside the quay, waving me off at the last minute. That would have been preferable to not having seen you at all because you hadn't shown up. Lateness, I could have forgiven...'

Suddenly, he took her hands in his and looked into her eyes. 'What happened was that I was on my way to see you off but there was a problem with the carriage wheel. I took the horse to try to get to you but had an accident where I banged my head. I woke up in this strange inn, barely being able to remember my own name for a couple of days...'

She let out a little gasp of surprise. 'I had no idea.'

'It was several days before I even got home again, and even then, my memory was cloudy. It's taken a long time for it to fully return. Then I remembered what had happened. So, you thought I'd abandoned you?'

She nodded slowly as realisation dawned. 'I'm afraid I did. I assumed as I'd turned down your proposal that you didn't want any more to do with me as you were so hurt by it. Oh, Archie, I should never have doubted you, but you broke my heart that afternoon...'

'So, how did you meet the good doctor?' He asked in a flippant manner.

She hesitated for a moment. 'On the journey, he was on his way back to New York...'

Archie swallowed. 'You didn't wait too long then and couldn't have been that heartbroken?' Then he felt like a heel as tears sprang to her eyes. He watched as she sobbed profusely. He had caused that upset and he chastised himself for upsetting the only woman he had really been in love with. He leaned over to hand her his silk handkerchief, closing the space between them, which she gratefully accepted.

'It wasn't like that at all. You won't believe what happened...' she sniffed. 'First of all, I discovered we were setting sail for New York and I hadn't a clue about it, and then I discovered that Nurse Carmichael had been overdosing my grandmother.' She let out a shuddering breath.

'I'm sorry to hear that.'

'It was such a shock.'

'But how did you discover that?'

'Hetty told me of her suspicions and we lay in wait to find out exactly what was going on. Apparently, Grandma's physician was behind it all. Once the medication was gradually tailed off, she became well again and more like the grandmother I'd always known. Sheldon had a friend at the hospital who is an expert on addictions, so she spent some time there being weaned off it.'

'And the nurse?'

'She was dismissed from taking care of Grandma and sent to the hospital to work as there was an outbreak of flu.'

'So, has she returned to England with you?'

Lucy shook her head. 'No, she realised she has burned her bridges working for my grandmother and has opted to remain in New York. She has no family and she seems to like it there.'

Archie nodded. 'So, when did you wed?'

'Just before the journey home.'

'And are you happy, Lucy?'

She lifted her eyes to look into his. 'I believe I am, yes.'

That's all he needed to know because all he cared about was her happiness. Taking her hand in his rather larger one, he gave it a little squeeze. 'Then I'm glad for you, truly I am, but I shall always hold a little piece of you in my heart, you're the final part of the jigsaw.'

She looked at him through glassy eyes trying to comprehend what he was saying to her but before he had time to explain, in the distance, Archie noticed Sheldon headed towards them and he quickly removed his hand from Lucy's. She was no longer his.

***

Archie noticed how Lucy's face blanched as Sheldon approached. Was she a little wary of her own husband, he wondered?

'Oh, there you are,' Sheldon said as if somewhat surprised to find them both in the garden, yet hadn't Adella already said she wanted Lucy to show him around it? He hadn't left them together for even a few minutes before he was back at his wife's side and sitting on the bench beside her, firmly taking her hand. It was then that the sight of how Lucy was with Sheldon, and the way he was with her, was beginning to remind him of ghosts from the past.

'Y...yes,' Lucy answered. 'Mother wanted me to show Archie the fountain.' Though in truth, neither of them had even got to see it as there was a lot to catch up on, but Archie felt the chance of being alone in her presence was fast fading away and now, maybe he'd never get another whilst she was back in England. His gut wrenched at the very thought that he might never get to see her again after this visit. Oh, she'd promise to visit for sure, but tickets to sail from New York to England would not be cheap. He swallowed hard trying to stop his eyes from filling with tears in front of the man who now seemed to be staring him out as if to say, *'You're an intruder, you're unwanted here. You're part of my wife's past and you no longer focus in her future.'*

Part of him felt like conceding defeat, though he was never one to give up, not even when he'd had that bully Ashcroft on his back years ago. No, he'd faced up to the opposition then and he could do it again now. Besides, he couldn't just make some excuse to leave that would be rude, particularly to Adella, his hostess, and of course to Lady Fanshaw who was waiting to see him.

But for now, he stood and said, 'If you'll both excuse me, I'll leave you to it for a moment as I need to see Lady Fanshaw.' His eyes met with Lucy's. She nodded and smiled, then Sheldon caught her attention, so she turned her gaze towards him as they conversed together. It was patently obvious to Archie that Lucy was attentive towards him and would make a fine doctor's wife.

He sighed to himself as he made his way back to the house as those ghosts of the past crept up on him.

Flora and Bill Brackley!

Chapter Twenty-two

1885

"Love's Labour's Lost"

Lucy glanced across the table at Archie, who was deep in conversation with her grandmother. Lady Fanshaw was becoming quite animated as she gesticulated wildly with her hands as she related tales about New York and their journey there and back to Archie. No detail was spared by the sound of it and she admired his patience for listening so attentively, many men wouldn't have, Sheldon for one. She had noticed how impatient and distracted he seemed lately, a far cry from that charming man she'd encountered on board the steamer ship. Ever since their marriage she'd witnessed another side to him. It was almost as though now they were wed—he didn't have to woo her anymore or charm her, either. Sometimes she wondered if she was just imagining this to be so, reassuring herself with the thought that married men and women's relationships wouldn't be in the hearts and flowers category any more. It was like this for many wives, especially for those whose husbands were married to their jobs like Sheldon was. Following an initial few nights of passion since their wedding day, he'd hardly touched her in that way since. Sometimes she ached for his touch at night in bed.

But she so liked his mother and had warmed to the thought of them marrying as she had no longer thought of a future with Archie. How foolish though! Why had she thought he would let her down like that? He never had done in the past, not even when they were children. It was then she realised that she had been swept off her feet and charmed by a man who wasn't what he purported to be. In fact, since their marriage he had become jealous and possessive, traits she hadn't realise he possessed before. He didn't want her in the bedroom but he didn't want anyone else to have her either, that much was evident. She made excuses for him by thinking he worked so hard at the hospital but surely that wouldn't account for his disregard of her?

Something Aunt Bessie had said to her once suddenly ran through her mind. *Marry in haste, repent at leisure.*

Momentarily, Archie looked across at her and their eyes locked. It was as if he could see into her very soul. She glanced away in case Sheldon should notice, but instead, he was in deep conversation with her mother. Why did Mother want to speak to him alone, anyhow? She'd said they had business to conduct. She felt as his wife that she should be privy to what that business was. Most certainly, it was not something that they deemed should concern her and she felt very out of things. Why shouldn't she know as yet? It was as if her mother and Sheldon held a secret that she couldn't be part of, and for some reason, it made her feel very jealous indeed. Just like Sheldon does, she told herself. He obviously felt threatened by Archie. And she supposed he should too because they both had a lot of history together. Now she had lost Archie forever and for that she was truly sorry. She had lied to him earlier about thinking she was happy now she was married, doing so to save face and she didn't want to upset him either. Archie was her one true love and now it was all too late.

***

A surge of guilt washed over Archie; he hadn't been paying as much attention to what Lady Fanshaw had to tell him about the trip since he'd noticed Lucy glancing at him every so often. Distracted by this, he'd picked up bits and pieces about what the woman told him about being hospitalised after what that "dreadful nurse" had done to her under doctor's orders and how she'd make sure her own physician, who was the man in question, should be taken to task over it before he caused any more problems for anyone else's life. And he'd heard all about their various trips to the grand shopping stores and art galleries she'd visited with Lucy.

But it was talk of the Sheldon household he listened to most intently. It was patently obvious to him that Sheldon's mother was a decent caring woman to have put them up in her home. But what about Sheldon himself? Was he really who he said he was: a respected New York doctor and an author to boot who had written about the improvised folk of Whitechapel? When Archie had questioned Lady Fanshaw about the book, she'd related that little nugget of information to him. It was then he realised he was looking for an excuse, any old excuse, to besmirch the man and tarnish his reputation so that Lucy could realise what he was before she made a decision to return to America with him.

No, Archie, you must not do this! A voiced heeded him.

It pulled him up sharp, as another voice said, *But you've met enough Sheldon sorts in your life to realise what he is. It's not just instinct. The man is a bully like Ashcroft was.* He'd seen the way Sheldon kept telling Lucy what to do and why did he have to speak with her mother behind her back like that? It was most rude in his book and goodness knew why Adella was going along with it.

He decided to find out more about the man whilst he spoke to Lady Fanshaw. 'So, you enjoyed staying at the house then?' He asked looking into her rheumy blue eyes for any flicker of consternation. But there was none. 'Oh, yes, indeed. Violet was very good to us.'

'And Sheldon?' he whispered.

'Pardon?'

He'd forgotten that sometimes Lady Fanshaw was hard of hearing and he couldn't risk raising his voice so everyone could hear him asking about Sheldon, who was just across the table. He glanced across at the man but he was in deep conversation with Lucy.

Deciding to take a risk he said, 'I expect Sheldon was good to you, too?'

'Oh yes, but he was hardly there for some of the time as he had to be called back to the hospital to live-in for some weeks when that flu epidemic took hold.'

So, she obviously didn't know the man as well as he'd thought, and neither could Lucy then in the matter of weeks she'd resided at his home.

A young maid brought in a large silver salver of salmon and set it down in the middle of the table, somehow Archie had lost his appetite. 'Archie,' Adella said suddenly, breaking his train of thought, 'You'll join us for Christmas day, won't you?'

Part of him would rather not do, but it might be his last chance to see Lucy before she left for America and slipped out of his life forever.

'Yes, I'd like that very much. Thank you for inviting me.' He glanced across the table at Sheldon whose face was giving nothing away, it was a blank canvas and that concerned him.

But right now, nothing nor no one could concern him as much as Lucy's happiness and to ensure himself all was well, he needed to check out what the man was up to.

After dining well on braised Salmon with seasonal vegetables followed by creme brulee, which was divine, Archie sat back in his seat and let out a little moan of satisfaction. The feast had been easier to digest than he'd previously thought. Maybe it was because he now had a plan in mind. He decided to visit the nearest library to check out that man and his so-called book. Maybe it would give him an insight into his life and behaviour if he were to read a few chapters. Get into his mind as it were.

After taking port in the drawing room with sherry for the ladies again, he made his excuses to leave. As he looked up at the striking portrait of the handsome Nathaniel Knight over the fireplace, he inwardly told the man he would watch out for Lucy's welfare. It would be the final thing he could do for him, the man who had helped Adella find her daughter again. The trouble was the woman seemed to be charmed by Sheldon so he could hardly say anything untoward about him to her. He didn't want to alienate her, so thereby having to stay away from the house. For time being he just had to play the game.

***

Archie made his way down the treelined street. It was icy underfoot that morning so he was careful to watch his step as he walked along. The small library was located above a solictor's office called *James Lingerwood and Sons*. According to Baxter, who was a fount of all knowledge, it was what was termed a lending library, where people were allowed to select books to take to their own homes for a couple of weeks. There was also a section known as a reference library. Uncertain where he should look first to find what he needed to know he asked a young female assistant if he might speak with the chief librarian there. The young lady, who had her hair styled in an elegant swept up fashion, nodded and said, 'Please could you wait a moment, sir, I'll see if she's busy.' She walked over to a heavy wooden door and rapped on it three times with her knuckles. 'Enter,' a deep sounding voice retorted. Expecting to see a man stood there, he was astonished to see that the voice had emanated from a middle-aged female who wore her salt and peppered coloured hair in a tight chignon knot. On her button nose balanced a pair of round gold coloured spectacles. Her sharp beady brown eyes seemed to be appraising him in one fell swoop, In fact she reminded him of an eagle. Or was it an owl? Whatever it was, if it was an eagle then she would be sharp and if an owl she would be very wise indeed, he decided.

'Can I help you, Mister er?' she peered over her spectacles.

'Pomfrey. Archie Pomfrey,' he explained.

Her eyes immediately lit up. 'Of course, I know the family and I heard about the fact Richard Pomfrey has a new son and heir. Indeed, I was saddened to hear of the deaths of your father and half-brother. You have my sincere condolences.'

Taken aback, he didn't quite know how to respond as he had never met either man though by now, he had heard a lot about both.

'I was wondering if you could let me know anything about a book written by an American gentleman named, Sheldon Harrington. Sorry Sheldon Harper Brown is his pen name, I believe. He's from New York. Apparently, he's an eminent physician there.'

She wrinkled her nose as if trying to bring the book and author to mind. 'Any idea of its title? That would help enormously…'

'I'm afraid I haven't, but it's about the impoverished people of Whitechapel if that's any help to you?'

She smiled at him. 'Indeed, it is. I'll check our records to see what I can find; it might take some time though. Meanwhile, I'll arrange for my assistant to make you a cup of tea. How does that suit?'

He nodded gratefully, but for the life of him didn't think that all visitors got such treatment from her. He guessed it was the name "Pomfrey" that opened such doors for him. Though he had never planned to exploit the name.

She gestured for him to take a seat and within a few minutes, the assistant returned with a cup of tea on a tray and a plate of biscuits for him, which he was glad of because he hadn't eaten breakfast before leaving the house that morning. He just wanted to delve into the life of Sheldon Harper Brown/Harrington or whoever he was, like a dog burrowed for its bone. Something was amiss and he wanted to find out what that something was. If living in Whitechapel as a youngster had taught him anything, it was to live off his wits and his instincts were screaming at him that the man was a scoundrel.

He had just placed his teacup on the side table, having finished it, when the librarian returned with a file under her arm. 'I've checked our records and indeed there was a book published just last month by a doctor called Sheldon Harper Brown, but I'm afraid the copy is out on loan to someone at the moment.'

He let out a low groan. *So near and yet so far!*

'Don't worry though, Mr Pomfrey, I've checked and it's due back today. As soon as it's been returned, I'll put it one side for you.'

He smiled, grateful that she was so accommodating. 'Thank you. What time would be best to call in?'

'Call about midday tomorrow that way we'll have had time to sort through any of today's returns,' she said.

As he left the library, he wondered what the book would reveal. He thought he'd take the time to browse around the shops for Christmas presents. If he was invited to Christmas dinner at Adella's home then he would need to purchase gifts. He had something special in mind for Lucy which was still in his desk drawer at home. But maybe he'd purchase a box of marzipan fancies for Adella as he knew she was partial to those and there was a confectioner's shop just across the road. Possibly he could select a sketch pad and brushes for Lady Fanshaw as she'd told him she was painting again these days since her hospital visit. But what about Sheldon? What could he give him? A bottle of port? A box of cigars? A punch in the face? He almost laughed out loud to himself as he took the stairs from the library out onto the street below. It was unsporting of him he realised that but the man had taken the only other woman, apart from his mother, that he'd really loved. His mother of course had been snatched away from him as a young lad and now it had happened with Lucy too, but in an entirely different way. Why did life have to be so cruel? He was so deep in thought that he almost failed to see the man who'd been on his mind, walking towards him, head down. He was about to say something in greeting even though the words would have caught in his throat, when Sheldon crossed the road and headed in a different direction to him. It was obvious he hadn't spotted Archie. It gave him the idea to follow after him.

***

The good doctor appeared to be headed towards an inn across the road, one with a dubious reputation. Why on earth would he head there? And why wasn't he at home with his wife? He waited a few minutes before following him inside the inn which was called *The Grouse and Peacock*. His eyes scanned the busy bar room for any sign of the man, but seeing none, he began to wonder if his eyes had initially deceived him and the fellow had taken a detour to the bakery next door? He was about to leave when a brazen looking barmaid, whose décolletage seemed to be spilling over the top of her low-cut bodice, faced him with an empty tray in her hand. 'Anything I can tempt you with, sir?' She asked and then tipped him a saucy wink. He could well guess her intentions but he needed to find out more.

'So, you have other services you can supply me with?' he dropped some coinage in her outstretched hand.

She nodded. 'We only offer the best-looking, well behaved gentlemen, mind. None of your riff raff are allowed upstairs, it's by order of the landlord.'

'And what are his orders?'

She tapped the side of her nose. 'Come with me and you'll find out.'

He couldn't believe that he could gain access to the upstairs area so easily, while other customers remained downstairs at the bar, blissfully unaware, sipping away at their pints of ale. Or maybe they did know, but realised that either they didn't fit the profile for the gentlemen's club upstairs or else they simply couldn't afford the entrance fee. After all, his Savile Row, well-tailored clothing, looked expensive and that's probably why he was allowed easy access to the place, he assumed.

He followed her to a little door at the back of the barroom. She turned suddenly, 'Take your cloak, sir?'

He shook his head. Who knew what might happen to it if he left it with her sort? 'Er no, thank you.'

'Ain't you a plummy sort an' all!' she retorted, rolling her eyes and throwing her hands up in mid-air as if he was giving her a hard time of it.

He smiled to himself. Plummy indeed! In fact, he was *her sort* once upon a time.

'Just climb them stairs and you'll see Jasmine at the top, she's one of the girls, she'll take care of you.'

He nodded, now feeling nervous at what was to happen up there. He'd never been to anywhere like this before. He knew men had particular needs even gentlemen, and some of those had trawled the streets of Whitechapel in search of women of easy virtue to give them thrills their wives at home couldn't or wouldn't do.

As he ascended the stone steps, he swallowed hard as Jasmine's silhouette came into view and as he reached the top step, she took a step back and he drew in a shuddering breath at just how beautiful she was. She wore a sheer lilac gown that was edged with lace, so sheer he could see the outline of her curvaceous breasts beneath. He was only a man after all and maybe some other time, he would be sorely tempted.

'Anything I can get for you, sir?' she asked in almost a shy way as she batted her eyelids. He guessed the landlord had coached her to act in a bashful fashion, but goodness knew how many men she had been servicing on the premises.

'I'd just like a little chat with you, that's all,' he whispered as he took some coins from his wallet and handed them her. She took them from his hand and slipped them in a small velvet drawstring bag which she then placed between her breasts for safe keeping, causing Archie's eyes to grow large with wonder.

'That's what they all tell themselves, that they just want to talk…' she said in a suggestive manner, 'but they all succumb to the charms of my girls in the end.'

'You mean, it's not er, how shall I put it, yourself who will take care of my needs?'

'Oh no, sir. I'm the overseer…'

He nodded. *More like the madam and now I'll need to part with even more money to get the confidential information I require.* But it would be worth it, he realised, to keep Lucy safe, if that information was vital for her welfare.

'I'll take you to Bella then. She's good with our first timers.'

He smiled. 'Please, lead the way…'

He followed her across the well-polished floor boards. The wall paper was embossed and looked expensive and velvety looking. A gasolier was suspended from the ceiling and a couple of oil lamps set on several low tables gave the landing a dim but sultry effect. A far cry from the raucous barroom downstairs.

At the end of the landing after passing a couple of doors, they arrived at a third, their final destination.

Softly, Jasmine rapped on the door and it swung open. There stood a petite young lady with olive skin and sparkling jade green eyes. She had almost a gypsy like appearance that he found very appealing. Her raven black hair hung in curls on her shoulders and her earlobes sported silver hooped earrings. She wore a black low-cut gown which appeared to be more of a night gown than a day one. He swallowed hard, realising she would be difficult to resist. The strong smell of perfume on her person was incredibly seductive and intoxicating to his senses.

Jasmine looked at him, expectantly. 'Does Bella meet with your requirements, sir?'

He nodded and smiled. 'She does indeed.'

'Then pay her half of the money upfront and half when you leave. I'm sorry we have to do it this way but it's…'

'Landlord's orders?' He arched an eyebrow.

'Yes, sir. You see our girls have been taken advantage of more than once.'

'It's quite all right. I understand perfectly.'

'Then I'll leave you both to it,' she said, closing the door behind herself as she left to stand attendance back at the top of the stairs.

Bella smiled at him. She had a wayward look about her as if she was all free and would make love with great abandonment, though it was not really what he was after right now. 'So, if you can pay me a shilling now and one afterwards, please.' She opened up her palm as he scrabbled in his wallet for another coin, which he dropped into her hand. She quickly placed it in the pocket of her dress.

'No, problem. I'll pay you for your time but I'm not after what you're offering.'

She frowned. 'Sorry, I don't understand?'

'It's information I want.'

'All right. But what can I tell you? The landlord don't want his business bandied about.'

'Please I can assure you, it's nothing like that. There's this man you see who has recently married a friend of mine and I'm very unsure about him. I just followed him in here. He's not downstairs so I guessed he might be up here with one of the girls.'

She wrinkled her nose. 'All right, but what's he like?'

'He's tall, about my height, well dressed. A toff.'

'Sounds just like you!' she chuckled.

'Yes, maybe. We do look a bit alike actually,' though he hated to admit it, 'but he could give me about ten years as he's in his thirties, he's also an American.'

'Well, bless me soul!' She sat on her bed and blinked in surprise. 'I do know who you mean though he calls himself *Mr Adams* whenever I see him. He's been here a few times since he arrived in England. Said he's visiting a friend but no mention of any wife. In fact, I just spotted him going into Dora's room. She's in to some unusual practices, if you get me drift!'

He nodded.

The good doctor's not wasting any time then! At least it confirmed something for him, the man wasn't who he purported to be.

Archie blew out a long breath, feeling so happy he wanted to punch the air, but he had to travel with caution, he realised that. To catch a mackerel, he needed a sprat. 'Can you tell me anything else?' He smiled, dropping another shilling into the girl's hand.

Chapter Twenty-Three

1885

"What's Going On?"

Lucy had a niggling feeling in the pit of her stomach. Her mother and Sheldon had seemed in cahoots again when they all took afternoon tea together. If she didn't know better, then she'd have thought there was something of a romantic nature going on between the pair—the whispering in corners and the shared jokes. Whenever she'd glanced over at them there appeared to have been *something* going on. She felt a sliver of guilt for thinking such an awful thing though. Yes, there might have been something going on behind her back but it was definitely not some sort of affair between them. Her mother had been deeply in love with Nathaniel, so for her to fall for someone so quickly would be out of character for her.

Still, Sheldon had been evasive since they'd arrived in England. She realised he had acquaintances in the country as he had once lived here for many months while he was researching his book about the people of Whitechapel, but who were these men who were keeping him out so late at night and during the day too? It seemed that not a day slipped by without him having to go somewhere or other. She was beginning to feel very lonely indeed.

She decided that when the time was right, she was going to get her mother on her own and ask her exactly what was going on between her and Sheldon. The opportunity presented itself later that evening before Sheldon had returned from one of his jaunts, supposedly to see an old friend who was a London doctor at some gentleman's club or another she had never even heard of before.

Grandmother had taken herself off to bed earlier than usual as she had a touch of a cold coming on, and Adella had insisted on putting her mother to bed herself after ordering Cook to prepare a hot rum toddy for the woman. Lucy well understood her mother's concern as she'd seen how ill Lady Fanshaw had become before they left for America, but she should now realise that the woman was back to normal now she was weaned off the laudanum.

Adella approached along the corridor, the wide skirts of her damask silk dress brushing against the wall, making a rustling sound. As she drew near to Lucy, she smiled widely at her daughter. 'Whatever's the matter, sweetheart?' she said, taking her daughter's face in both hands. 'You look as if the weight of the world is on your shoulders?'

Lucy stepped back in anger. 'I was hoping you could tell me!' she said, trying to contain her emotion at the situation.

Adella's eyes widened in confusion. 'Look, whatever it is, I'm sure we can solve this over a chat and a cup of coffee in the drawing room,' her mother said softly.

Lucy nodded. There was no point in upsetting the woman, she'd been through so much lately.

As they walked the corridor with Adella in front of her daughter, the silence was palpable and the atmosphere tense.

Why my husband, Mama? Is it because you lost your own and now need another man to lean on?

Releasing a long breath, Lucy followed her mother into the drawing room, then closed the door behind them. There was a roaring fire and both sat in an armchair near it, facing one another. Adella rang a little brass bell and summoned the maid to order a pot of coffee for them.

'Macaroons, Lucy?'

'Er, no thanks.'

Adella addressed the maid. 'That'll be all, Peggy. Thank you. Just make sure the coffee is nice and hot this time.'

The maid nodded and curtseyed before leaving the room. Lucy marvelled at how sweet her mother was even when ticking the young girl off for delivering stone cold coffee the previous time.

'Well, now then. Do tell me how I can help you?' her mother said warmly, making Lucy's temper slowly dissipate into thin air. Adella had the knack of soothing troubled waters with her softly spoken voice and calm demeanour.

'I've noticed lately how you and *my husband* seem to be whispering in corners together…'

'You have? Oh, my! And you think there is something going on between us?' Adella's eyebrows lifted in surprise.

'No,' Lucy shook her head. 'Not exactly that…but there's something going on that I don't feel part of.'

Adella chewed on her bottom lip. 'Oh Lucy, there's nothing bad going on, believe me.'

'Then just what is it? Please tell me.' To Lucy's horror, tears filled her eyes.

'Please don't cry, my darling. I'm only confiding in him regarding financial matters that's all.'

Lucy blinked several times through misted eyes. 'But why him, why not someone else?'

'I have to confess I've never been much good with money. Years ago, Mother took care of all that, then as you know I was in that mental institution so I had no need to take care with it. Then I married Nathaniel and he was good at that sort of thing. Oh Lucy, when he died, he left such a lot of paperwork for me to deal with: potential investments, savings funds and so on. I'm quite flummoxed by it all.' Her mother looked genuinely distraught.

'You're not in any financial difficulties though are you, Mother?'

'Oh no, good heavens. It's quite the reverse. Nathaniel's left a lot of money behind in the form of property and land. But I don't know where to begin to sort it all out. One night when you went to bed early, I sat and chatted with Sheldon and shared my concerns with him. He told me he knows a broker in the city of London who can help me out with regards to how I can invest the money wisely.'

Lucy nodded. 'Have you parted with any money as yet?'

'Oh no, nothing like that. I've just given Sheldon some deeds and other financial documents for the broker to take a look at should I care to employ him.'

'I think I understand.' Though she didn't really. Why should her mother go behind her back to trouble Sheldon with such things? Then she felt bad for thinking that way, her mother had always been a fragile little thing since being a young girl, she was too young at heart and delicate for this world. No wonder she had asked Sheldon as he had seemed someone trustworthy and in the know with his contacts.

'I was just thinking though, why you didn't ask Archie instead as you've known him for years?' Lucy studied her mother's face for an answer.

Adella nodded. 'He would seem the obvious choice as he has the backing of his uncle, but I thought as you and he had parted on such strange terms…When you sent me that letter saying how upset you'd been after he'd let you down that day you left England, I feared he might not be as trustworthy as either of us initially thought. You see, I'd thought you'd already said your goodbyes when you visited him that previous afternoon, I had no idea he'd promised to be there with the rest of us when you boarded the ship. I felt let down on your behalf, Lucy.'

Lucy blinked back tears. 'I am so sorry I ever thought that way to begin with. I honestly think if I hadn't met Sheldon on that ship my mind and heart would still have been with Archie. I'm afraid that Sheldon swept me off my feet.'

Adella smiled as her eyes shone as she spoke. 'I can see how that might happen; he is most charming. You are very fortunate to be married to such a wonderful man.'

Before she had a chance to utter another word, the maid returned with the tray of coffee.

'Thank you, Peggy. Just set it down on the occasional table there.' The maid did as instructed and then left the room.

Adella poured the coffee into the awaiting cups, her hands trembling slightly as she did so.

Have I upset you, Mama? I do hope not.

Lucy pushed that thought away before firmly saying, 'I can see now why you asked Sheldon to help you but you should have included me as his wife, Mama. Not kept me in the dark.'

Adella nodded. 'You're absolutely correct, Lucy. I've been assuming you wouldn't be at all interested. I never wanted to get concerned in Nathaniel's financial affairs and thought you would be the same as me, not wanting to know about monetary issues. I am so sorry—will you forgive me?'

Lucy warmed to the woman, 'Of course I will.'

All of this was very well but it still didn't explain Sheldon's long absences from the house. Lucy took the cup of coffee from her mother's outstretched hand. At least she now knew the state of play and she'd be watching her husband with a keen eye in future.

***

Archie decided to abandon his Christmas shopping for another day. He just couldn't concentrate after what he'd been told. So, Sheldon had visited that bordello above the barroom several times lately. He had partaken of sinful activities with at least two of the girls there on various occasions—both Bella and Dora. How could he do something like that when he had a beautiful young wife like Lucy at home? He felt so mad he wanted to punch the man's lights out. He'd say nothing for time being, not until he had gathered more evidence. He still wanted to find out about that book too. When he had all he needed to present, then he'd tell Lucy and not behind Sheldon's back either, but in front of the man.

That night he barely slept a wink as things rolled over in his mind. He needed to get that library book in his hands and go over it with a fine toothcomb. At precisely five minutes to midday he presented himself at the library again. The young assistant, looking as elegant as ever, was behind the counter flipping through a wooden tray of what appeared to be small index cards. She was deep into her work, so he coughed to clear his throat, causing her to drop her task in hand and turn to face him with a smile. 'Yes, sir?' She blinked.

'The chief librarian told me to call today for a book that was due to be returned yesterday. She said she would put it to one side for me...' he said as his breath caught in his throat.

For a moment, he had a feeling that the book hadn't been returned as there was a long silence and then the girl's hazel eyes illuminated with recognition. 'Oh, yes. Miss Bradley and I have been discussing the book this morning,' she said, hardly able to contain her excitement. 'Apparently, you're a friend of the author?'

'Oh, I wouldn't say friend exactly but he's married to someone who is a friend of mine.'

That seemed enough for the girl as she seemed to fawn in the reflective glory of knowing someone who knew an author who had written a mighty fine book.

'What's so special about the book, then?' he asked curiously.

'The doctor made lots of observations when he wrote it and it's become both a British and American classic piece of work of human observation of poverty and neglect in the poorer classes of society, much has been learned from it,' she said proudly, almost as if she had practised those words by heart so she could tell visitors to the library about the book.

He leaned in towards the wooden counter. 'But something I can't quite comprehend; how did he get so close to the people of the area?' He understood all too well how distrusting the people could be towards outsiders, particularly someone who looked like a gentleman in fine clothing.

She leaned in herself across the desk, almost in a conspiratorial fashion as she whispered, 'He posed as one of them. He bought tattered old clothing from a dolly shop and pretended he needed a room for the night. He ended up staying at several doss houses and inns. He even picked up some casual work in some places to keep himself fed.'

'Didn't anyone even guess, particularly as he had an American accent?'

'No, Miss Bradley told me she had a quick read of the first couple of chapters when it was returned today. He describes himself as a master of languages, having the ability to copy any accent. No one suspected a thing!'

'Utterly amazing!' Archie stood back with wide eyes and rubbed his smooth freshly shaven chin. He was about to pose another question, when a customer arrived who appeared to be in a hurry. The gentleman was middle aged and well dressed in a black woollen frock coat and felt bowler hat, appearing every inch a city gent who was probably on his break from the office.

'Please see to this gentleman,' Archie said kindly, moving aside.

The man nodded at him in appreciation and stepped forward to place two library books on the counter.

He was quickly seen to as the assistant took his cardboard library card from his hands and recorded the date they were due back on in her ledger and inside both books. The gentleman was soon on his way, tipping his hat to the pair of them as he departed with his books tucked under his arm.

'Miss Bradley says she's going to read the whole book when you return it,' the assistant said, turning her attention back to Archie. 'Then I'd like to read it after her, it always pays to keep abreast of such matters.'

'Yes, it does indeed.'

'And fancy you knowing the author. How often have you met him?'

'Once or twice. As a matter of fact, I'll be dining with him again on Christmas day.'

At that point, Archie wondered if he'd gone too far as the girl's face flushed and he thought for a moment she'd pass out from the excitement of it all. Smiling, he said, 'The book?'

'Oh, yes, the book. I'll fetch it for you now, sir.'

She returned within moments with a red book in her hands, cradling it to her bosom as if it were the most precious of goods. Then she placed it on the counter. Its title read "The Fire and Brimstone Folk".

'Thank you,' he said. 'Interesting title?'

'Yes, apparently he wanted to convey how living in the East End was akin to living in hell.'

Archie nodded, he couldn't disagree with that. For some in the area, Whitechapel was hell on earth.

He thanked her for her time and left with the book neatly tucked under his arm. On the coach ride home he opened the first page which read:

Dear reader, are you prepared to meet with the destitute? The waifs and strays of society? The weepers and the wailers who crawl through the abyss on their hands and knees, scratching for a bite to eat and a bed to rest their weary heads while you sleep soundly in your own? If so, come with me on a journey. Your journey will be in the imagination whilst mine was in taken in the flesh as I posed as one of their own sons. The dens of iniquity are real and remain to this day and the sins of the fathers are revisited on the children, some who don't even make it to their adult years. Teeming with pimps, prostitutes and pick pockets, let me walk you through the East End and the streets of Whitechapel…A metropolis of misery.

Archie let out a gasp. This man, if his work were his own, could write well. He felt immediately drawn in by the words that Sheldon must have penned so carefully. But a little voice warned him, *If you as someone who is wise to this world, can be so easily drawn in, then so can others…*

Archie continued to read well after returning home. He cancelled dinner that evening, instead arranging for Baxter to ask Cook to send up a bowl of nourishing beef and vegetable soup and a hunk of bread along with a bottle of Corsican red wine. If Baxter was curious as to what his master was up to, he wasn't saying so and Cook knew better than to ask too.

He pored over the book until his eyes grew dry and weary. Could this really be the voice of the same Sheldon Harper Brown who he'd recently met? It would appear so. He was beginning to see the man in a new light. He rubbed his eyes and carried on reading.

I trawled the streets until the sky above became an inky dark blanket peppered with shining stars that first night.

An American gentleman in the East End of London, who if I should turn in any one direction and walk for just a few minutes would meet once again with the same sort of down trodden folk that I'd previously encountered in the opposite direction. Faces tinged with grease and grime, eyes hollow and haunted. The sounds of babies' cries from behind dirty, dusty window panes and even once from a long dark alley way, echoing along the abyss. Raucous shouts and leers from pubs on every corner, stenches that permeated my nostrils and turned my stomach over so that on occasion I wretched, but nothing came up. I wanted to be one of them, so I had eaten little since breakfast the previous day...

So, Sheldon had gone as far as even starving himself? It was just incredible that he would do such a thing.

I finally gave away my last few farthings to an elderly woman who sat hunched on the pavement, cradling a young child to her bosom. Despite the biting cold, the woman sat there wrapping her flannel shawl well around herself and the child, who appeared to be asleep. On second look, she wasn't elderly at all, beneath the golden glow of the lamp light I could see she was no more than thirty years old; her previous demeanour had made her appear old before her time. She looked up at me as I dropped the coins into her grubby palm and mouthed a 'Thank you!' Then she quickly snapped shut the palm of her hand as if fearful someone might see and scrabbled to hide the coins in the pocket of her skirt. Now I really was one of them. I had no money, an empty belly and no shelter for the night. What was I to do now?

Archie let out a long breath, feeling ashamed that he might have misjudged the man, but even so, if he had lived as one of Whitechapel's own, why was he treating his wife so appallingly? He knew he wouldn't rest until he'd read right through the book.

During his reading time, amongst which he sent for a pot of strong coffee to keep himself awake after imbibing the wine, he learned many things. Sheldon had lived off his wits in Whitechapel. He'd somehow managed to wangle entry to the workhouse and described it as *A questionable place where the weeping and wailing echoed from every wall...* A visit to a doss house was described as: *Every man was for himself. A hunk of bread and cheese with a hot cup of tea is one thing, but sleeping in hard pine beds in close proximity to one another in multiple lines, reminded me of a row of coffins at the local undertakers' parlour! Make no bones about it, many of my contemporaries would end there soon enough living that unfortunate lifestyle. And to awake in the morning without losing one's possessions from light fingers, would make one very fortunate indeed. That's if you'd manage to sleep at all as some nefarious sorts roll up fuelled up by alcohol and ready to fight over anything: a cross word, a neighbour's snoring, to be looked at in the wrong way. A better sleep could be had in the alleyway outside if it were not for the rats as large as cats...*

On and on he read as the doctor described the people and their various ailments and how a couple actually died before his very eyes, it made for a harrowing read. *The population exploded here with the influx of people from Ireland and Eastern Europe. It's now every man and every woman for themselves as people tout for casual work. There is just so much competition. The young seamstress who works sixteen hours a day at the local slop shop and can hardly stay awake at times...she provides a meagre income, but woe betide she should lose her occupation as some have been known to end up as "The Unfortunates". Nymphs of the pave or in simple terms, they end up prostituting themselves for a crust of bread. Where once she was sewing petticoats for the slop shop now, she's lifting her own for sordid purposes. And what of the dockers who queue up on a daily basis to see if they will be selected for work that day? Woe betide them if they look too old or inept? They're bound for the scrap heap. And the factory workers who work under hazardous conditions with hardly any breaks, what of those? The matchgirls who work with dangerous phosphorous, the tanners who work with vats of dye? No wonder the area is full of poverty, pestilence and despondency when the people are offered so little but give so much in return, even their lives at times. What chance do any of them have when there is so much overcrowding in the area?*

This was nothing new to Archie as he had once lived as they did for some time but it didn't hurt to be reminded of it. He felt a huge fat tear roll down his cheek and took his handkerchief from his waistcoat pocket to blot it away. Damn the man, he'd got under his skin and reminded him of a painful time in his own life. Still, it was well written though.

Sheldon went on to compare the area to somewhere else he knew in New York. Archie was about to close the book and put it down as a damn good read, when he noticed a final page as he flipped what he thought had been the final one. It was an author biography and a pen and ink style sketch of the author himself.

Archie's mouth gaped open. No wonder Sheldon's book had been so good and it had pulled at Archie's heartstrings! The author picture was of a much older man with a bald head and handlebar moustache, most definitely not the Sheldon he'd been introduced to. He scanned the biography:

Sheldon Harper Brown was born in New Hampshire in 1825. Which would make him sixty years old! The biography went on to say how he'd been happily married for forty of those years and had five children and all about his medical training. Nowhere did it explain him as being a thirty something (single man as he would have been penning that novel.)

Come on then, Sheldon? How are you going to explain this one?

Chapter Twenty-Four

1885

"Archie Visits an Old Friend"

Lucy's stomach lurched. She had just eaten breakfast and had been all right not long before that. Was she sickening for something? She pulled herself up off her bed where she'd been resting and dashed over to the cabinet. Removing the wash jug from inside the enamel bowl, she heaved her heart up into the bowl. Thank goodness she hadn't messed up her mother's lovely new oriental rug, she'd never have forgiven herself. When the heaving ceased, she took a couple of deep breaths and let them out again to keep any more sickness at bay. Then taking a clean towelling flannel from the vanity unit, she plunged it into the water jug to wash the debris from her face. Hopefully it was the kippers at breakfast that had disagreed with her and it wouldn't be a stomach bug. Strange, she felt perfectly fine now as if the sickness had never happened to her at all.

There was a soft knock on the bedroom door. Then her mother opened the door to peer inside with great concern on her face.

'Are you all right, Lucy?' she asked, walking towards her.

Lucy nodded. 'You heard me?'

'Yes, I'm afraid I did. I was in the bedroom next door giving orders to Hetty.'

Lucy groaned at the thought that even Hetty might have heard her heaving up. 'It must have been the kippers,' she said, rubbing her perspiring brow.

'No, I don't think so. I ate the same thing as you and I'm perfectly fine. But have you considered something else?'

'No, no,' said Lucy, shaking her head. 'It couldn't possibly be that already.'

'Look, come and sit down,' said her mother gently. She did as told, and her mother sat beside her draping her arm around her. 'You might not wish to think you're pregnant as yet, but it's perfectly possible. You'd been married for a month and staying here now for almost another month. All I'm saying is take it easy, just in case. When did you last see your courses?'

She fought to think for a moment. 'A few weeks since, but I've never been all that regular.'

'Well keep an eye on yourself, just in case.'

It wasn't just that there might be a baby involved now but Sheldon's behaviour was distressing her, and her grief over her stepfather's death. How could she be pregnant though? Her husband had barely touched her since their wedding night.

Without saying a word, her mother hugged her to her bosom, so Lucy felt safe and protected. After she had stopped crying, she lifted Lucy's chin with her thumb and forefingers and looked deep into her daughter's watery eyes. 'I wish I had been able to do this with you when you were a baby instead of abandoning you like I did. Please don't be upset about a pregnancy, your child won't miss out having you as a mother.'

'It's not that, Mama. It's Sheldon. He's out all the time lately. I hardly see him at all.'

'But from my understanding, he's visiting old friends and catching up with medical acquaintances…' Her mother stared at her for the longest time as if only now realising her daughter's fears and that maybe they were founded.

Lucy silently shook her head. 'I…I think there's something odd going on.'

'I'm so sorry, Lucy. I should have realised the way he's been out such a lot, how it might be affecting you, instead of leaving you to your own devices like I've been doing. I've been so wrapped up in my grief at having lost your stepfather that I've forgotten about anything else.'

'What do you think I ought to do, Mama? You had such a good marriage to Nathaniel, didn't you? I always hoped ours could be the same.'

'Yes, I did indeed,' she said as a light illuminated her eyes as she spoke of her husband in that manner, for the first time since Lucy had returned home. 'Let me think about that one.'

They sat in silence for a moment, then Mama said, 'I think you need to sit down with your husband and tell him just how lonely you're feeling lately. I never had any secrets from your stepfather and that's why our marriage worked so well.'

Lucy nodded. It was a good idea but she didn't hold up much hope for Sheldon telling her what was really going on with him, else she felt he would have done so by now. Day by day she felt she was losing him. Who was this man she had married? She hardly recognised him at all.

***

'But I didn't even know that Lucy was back in England!' Bessie Harper smacked the palm of her hand down heavily on the well-scrubbed pine table before her.

'Sorry.' Archie realised he should have told the elderly lady well before now but he'd just had too much on his mind lately. The woman had been so good to them both, he still thought of her like a wise old aunt, even though they weren't even related. She had been there for him in his hour of need.

They were both seated in Bessie's warm and homely kitchen and he had come to tell her about the death of Nathaniel Knight, who Bess had been really fond of as the man had helped her so much without her even realising it when Lucy was a nipper. A ginger tom cat lay curled up in a wicker basket in the corner near the range for warmth, whilst a large pile of dishes were stacked up near the wooden sink ready to be washed.

'Are you on your own these days then, Bess?' Archie wanted to know. He'd hate to think of the woman being alone now at her time of life. Although he thought of her as elderly, of course she was nearing her sixties or was she just mid-fifties? He wasn't sure, she had always seemed world weary and down trodden to him. Yet, she had turned her life around by throwing out that scoundrel of a husband, and then her pie business really took off.

'Well, yer'd think I was on me own with the ruddy mess around 'ere lately with that new kitchen 'elp I've taken on, the gal is bone idle!' She let out a little sardonic chuckle.

'Oh, no, it's not mess I'm bothered about. I haven't come to take a look at that. It's you I'm bothered about. With Christmas coming up, I'd have thought you'd have been invited up to the big house by Adella?'

She shook her head. 'No, lad,' she had a habit of still referring to him as a lad even after all these years. 'Wouldn't wish to impose now that Mr Knight has passed away. I didn't realise until you called.'

'Why on earth should you have realised? You don't really move in those sorts of circles, if you don't mind me saying so. It's not as if you even read *The Times* obituary section, is it?'

The woman shook her head slowly. 'Wouldn't have the time for it, with me pie business, not that I can't afford to buy a bloomin' newspaper, mind you!'

Oh dear, had he gone and upset her, but then she chuckled and said, 'No wonder Lucy's back home then but I'd have thought she'd have been in touch by now.'

'Didn't she even write to you while she was away?'

'Nope. Not one letter or postcard,' she said sadly. 'How long has she been back home for?'

'About three or four weeks.' Archie could see the disappointment etched on the woman's face as she let out a loud, shuddering sigh. So, he wasn't the only person Lucy hadn't bothered contacting on her overseas jaunt.

'But there's something else you should know, Bess…'

'Really?' For the first time he noticed the twinkle in her rheumy eyes.

'Lucy married an American doctor while she was over there.'

'What?' The cup of tea Bessie held in her hand almost toppled out of it. Slowly, she set it straight in its saucer back on the table.

'Yes. Really.'

'How come though? I thought she'd gorn to The Continent with her grandmother?'

'That was the original plan, yes. They ended up instead setting sail to New York and Lucy didn't realise it at first.'

'Well, she's a fast worker, I'll give her that. Been away less than six months and returned with a gold band on her finger!' She folded her hands on her lap and pursed her lips as she often did when she was annoyed or irritated by something. Then shaking her head in a solemn fashion said, 'Marry in haste, repent at leisure. I know that meself only all too well! In fact, no one knows that better than me. But I'd have thought she'd at least 'ave written to tell me about it even if I couldn't attend the wedding. I brought that gal up as if she were me own flesh and blood, Archie.'

He noticed tears in her eyes and reached out to pat her hand in reassurance. 'It wasn't like that. By all accounts, it was a whirlwind romance. They met onboard the ship as it sailed over. He'd been staying in England. She and her grandmother were invited as guests to his home and then he asked her to marry him.'

Bessie fell silent for a moment. 'You know, Archie,' she looked into his eyes, 'I once held hopes that she'd marry you!'

He smiled. 'So did I, Bess. In fact, I asked Lucy to get engaged before she left these shores, but she turned me down.'

Bessie's mouth fell open. 'How come? Weren't you good enough for her?'

'She said she couldn't possibly marry me as she was going overseas with Lady Fanshaw. You see she had a good reason at the time. It was thought that her grandmother was terminally ill, turns out she wasn't really. To make matters worse, she was waiting for me to say goodbye to her at the quayside that day but something happened beyond my control and I didn't make it to the dock in time.'

'Oh, you poor lad.' Bessie shook her head.

'Lucy took it that I just didn't care enough I suppose.'

'After you'd proposed to her an' all.' The cat chose that moment to leave its basket and jump on Bessie's lap. She smiled and sat there stroking his head as he purred softly in contentment.

Archie appeared deep in thought for a moment. 'Yes, but don't you see?'

Bessie shook her head. 'No?''

'She must have thought my not showing up was a deliberate act on my part as she'd turned me down and that somehow I was expressing my anger by not showing up that day.'

'Aye, maybe, Lad. But sometimes it doesn't do to dwell and try to analyse these things. Things happen for a purpose some times. Happen she was meant to marry the good doctor!'

'Believe me, Bess, there's nothing good about him at all.' Archie tutted beneath his breath.

'What did you say, Archie?' The cat suddenly sprang off Bessie's lap and returned to its basket as if somehow affronted by what Archie had said. Bessie cupped her ear and leaned in closer as if she had misheard him.

He was about to say "nothing" but then decided to confide in her. 'Between you and I, Bess…I'm concerned for Lucy's welfare living with that doctor.'

Bessie screwed up her features in puzzlement. 'How do you mean? Sure yer not just jealous of him, Lad?'

Archie felt his face flame red hot. 'Er, no. I mean, yes, of course I am but it's not that. At least that's not the main reason for my concern. The real reason is because I fear the man is a confidence trickster, a bounder, a cad.'

Bessie shook her head. 'But how can yer possibly be sure of that? Yer bound to have special feelings for her as yer've always been so close.'

Archie knew this was more than feelings, his intuition was so strong on this one. It was almost as though his inner voice was screaming at him to take Lucy to place of safety. It reminded him of the time Bill Brackley was after her back in Whitechapel. That had been a dreadful time and she'd have been pushed into prostitution if he hadn't warned her and led her to safety.

'Let me explain. I'd heard that he'd recently had a book published as a so-called, respected medical person from New York. Apparently, he went undercover in Whitechapel to study how the impoverished live.'

'Oh?' Bessie chewed on her bottom lip as if remembering her own sorry circumstances back in the day. He realised this was all so close to home for the pair of them and maybe she wouldn't like to dredge up the past, but even so, he needed to tell it how it was.

'My instincts warned me about the man, as soon as I met him to be honest with you. I made a visit to the library and the chief librarian managed to obtain a copy of the book for me. Apparently, it's a well-respected tome, newspaper articles have even been written about it and it was serialised in a New York newspaper as they have a similar area there. Sheldon compared Whitechapel to that area. I read right through the entire book in one night, even staying up late to do so. I was well impressed by what the man had done and with his style of writing.'

'So?'

'So, when I got to the final page, I noticed there was one I'd almost missed at the end of the book as the pages were stuck together. I managed to ease it gently open to discover that there was a biography printed about Sheldon Harper Brown, a sketch of him too.'

Bess angled her head to one side in puzzlement. 'He has the name of Harper like me.'

'Yes, but it's not his name, not even his pen name, as the name belongs to another.'

Now Bessie was shaking her head as if she couldn't quite fathom things out.

'Only you see it wasn't the same man who I'd been introduced to!'

Bessie gasped. 'Heavens above!' Her hand went to her chest as if she were wounded and Archie guessed her reaction was one of fear for Lucy. 'So, you mean the man you met, the same man who married our Lucy, is a fraud?'

Archie nodded. 'Yes. That's what it amounts to. Not only that, I saw him in the street after leaving the library. He didn't notice me, so I followed him...'

'Go on,' she urged as if impatient he'd paused mid-sentence.

'He ended up going inside an inn, though it wasn't just any old inn.'

'A gambling den?'

'No, a house of ill repute. I even managed to wangle my way upstairs. I had to pay for access, though of course, I did not partake of the wares those "ladies" had to offer but I did find out something—our dear doctor has been making regular visits there since arriving in England and has done so in the past whenever he visited the country.'

Bessie shook her head. 'Poor Lucy. That man is a dirty devil and a con artist. Why do you think he married her?'

'Isn't it obvious? She will inherit great wealth as when Lady Fanshaw passes away her money will pass on to Adella as the woman's daughter, then finally to Lucy. Adella, of course, also has her own fortune from her husband but Lady Fanshaw confided in me at a recent dinner party where I met that scoundrel, that she was planning on giving Lucy a sizeable sum to set her up as a newly wed.'

'Oh, my goodness!' Bessie said.

'He's charmed the Lady by the look of it. He had helped her to get back to good health by taking her to a physician friend of his. He is a real doctor but not the one we thought he was.'

Bessie looked at him with great concern. 'Oh dear, Archie, what are we going to do?'

'I really don't know, Bess…' Archie said sadly, 'but we have to do something.'

Bessie rose from her chair and laid a reassuring hand on his shoulder. 'I'll put the kettle on and we'll have another cuppa to discuss what we shall do about this.'

Archie looked up and smiled at her. Bess was a tower of strength, especially in a crisis.

***

It was late when Lucy heard a coach draw up outside the house. She peered through the lace of the bedroom curtains to see Sheldon alight from the coach and stagger across the drive way to the front door. The pair of hounds Nathaniel had kept as guard dogs, started to bark furiously. 'Blast you, Sheldon. Now you'll awaken the whole household…' she muttered under her breath.

She grabbed her dressing gown from the hook on the back of the bedroom door and quickly put it on, making her way across the landing.

Staring down the staircase into the dimly lit hallway, she saw the tall silhouette of her husband in his top hat and cape. A proper gentleman, or so it seemed to everyone else. Not wanting to disturb anyone, she descended the stairs, where he seemed surprised to see her.

'Sheldon, why are you creeping in at this early hour? Do you realise what time it is?' She became aware of how shaky her voice sounded.

'No, the night just slipped away…'

'It's a quarter past three. Now I demand to know what you've found to do all of this time?'

'I was at the club conducting a little business with one or two acquaintances and then we went on to a card game at another club.'

'A gambling one?'

'Yes. There's no crime in that, is there? It's not as if I've lost the shirt off my back or anything. It's the way business is conducted between gentlemen.'

Holding her chin in the air, she said, 'I'm really disappointed in you since we wed. You haven't had much time for me.'

'Look, let's go somewhere where we won't be overheard.' He led her to the drawing room. 'Please sit down, honey.'

A shaft of light illuminated the room, but he lit an oil lamp as she seated herself so they could see more clearly. Kneeling down beside her, he said, 'It's not what you think. I'm doing this for your mother.'

'My mother? What on earth does she have to do with you keeping late hours?'

'The gentleman I spoke to tonight, he's an investor. He has said he can take care of her finances by making various investments with her money.' That seemed to confirm what her mother had told her.

She nodded slowly. 'And just who is the gentleman you refer to?'

'I'm not at liberty to say anything as yet until it's officially confirmed and your mother has signed the various documentation.'

Lucy wasn't used to dealing with such things and Sheldon was, maybe she had got things all wrong these past few weeks? He had just been doing business with a few drinks and the odd wager of bets thrown in. In any case, she'd find out soon enough when her mother went to sign the necessary documents. A thought occurred to her, who did she trust most in the whole wide world who could give her advice?

Archie!

'Lucy, you've gone dreadfully quiet. Is anything the matter?'

Slowly, she shook her head. 'No, it's all right. I can see now what you're saying and I'm sorry for doubting you, Sheldon.'

He smiled. 'I'll tell you what, I'll take you anywhere you want, just the two of us.'

Brightening up she said, 'All right. How about we go to the tea room in Crownley tomorrow and maybe we can go Christmas shopping together afterwards?'

'Splendid.' Then he paused thoughtfully as he rubbed his chin. 'But can we make it the following day?'

Lucy shrugged. Her husband was a hard man to pin down but maybe he had her best interests at heart and those of her mother. It just wouldn't hurt one little bit to speak to Archie though. She missed him dreadfully. 'Yes, that's absolutely fine,' she said, forcing a bright tone to her voice. There was no point in alarming her husband. She really wasn't happy that he was not around as much as he could be. Tomorrow would be a good time then to visit her old friend. They hadn't had much time to chat when he'd called to the house. In fact, he'd spent more time chatting to her grandmother than to her. But then again, could she possibly blame him as her recent marriage must have been a shock for him?

Standing, she kissed her husband on his cheek. 'I'm off to bed.'

'I won't be long, I'll be up soon, honey,' he said making his way to an occasional table where he lifted the crystal decanter to pour himself a glass of brandy. That was another thing that concerned her, he drank too much alcohol for her liking. Goodness knew how long he'd stay down here drinking for.

'Night,' she said, making her way towards the door.

'Goodnight.'

She felt her heart slump as she realised he was far more interested in pouring himself a brandy than even looking at her to say goodnight.

***

Much to Lucy's surprise, Sheldon was up and dressed before she'd risen the following morning. He said little to her during breakfast. Mama and Grandma would be breakfasting later as they tended to begin the day later these days. Lucy knew that a darkness had descended on her mother as she'd heard her weep uncontrollably in the bedroom she'd once shared with Nathaniel. Grandmother had told Lucy it was best to leave her mother cry it out and not to intrude on her grief as it was only nature's way. Grandmother had endured her own share of grief when her own husband had passed away, so Lucy figured she knew what she was speaking about.

Most of breakfast was in silence as Sheldon leafed through the newspaper, only putting it down when his kippers and slices of bread and butter were served up by Hetty. Then he smiled charmingly at the girl. Who would have guessed that she felt so cut off from her own husband? Back in Auburn things hadn't felt that way at all, indeed, she'd felt close to him then, as if they were meant to be together. Where had it all gone wrong? It was as if the journey across the Atlantic had somehow changed him into his evil twin, but that couldn't possibly be so. She realised at that moment that she had been blind to the real Sheldon all along. He'd only shown her what he'd wanted her to see and now they were married, he didn't much care as she was now his property.

How could she have been so foolish?

Finishing the last morsel of his meal, Sheldon wiped his mouth with a linen napkin and tossing it onto the table, announced, 'I'm off to the city today…'

Lucy quirked an eyebrow. 'Oh?' She had realised he was going out of course as he'd told her so, but to the city?

'Yes, more business on your mother's behalf as she's not in a fit state to do these things for herself.'

She should have been grateful, she supposed, but somehow it didn't sit right with her.

He took a last swig of tea from his china cup before settling it back down on its saucer.

'Shall I pour you another?' She realised she was doing anything she could possibly do to keep him with her, even for a few minutes longer, but it was of no use. It was obvious he had more pressing plans which didn't include her.

'No, I need to be there on time, these things won't wait.'

He rose and pushed his chair back in towards the table. Automatically, as he approached her, she proffered her cheek, but instead he took her hand and kissed it as she felt his moustache brush the back of her hand. Wasn't he even going to kiss her on the face any more? She wondered if she should tell him that she might be carrying his baby? But she wasn't sure, she hadn't vomited following breakfast this past couple of days, so maybe it had all been in her imagination anyhow.

'What time shall I see you later?' she blinked.

'If I'm not back by dinner, don't wait up for me, you'll know things have gone on a bit longer than normal.'

Dinner? That was hours away, but then again, she told herself it would take some time for him to get to the city and back again. So instead she said, 'Have you arranged for the carriage to be ready for you?'

'Yes, I arranged that last night. I asked the hansom that brought me home to return at half past eight today for me.'

'You didn't ask Mother for the use of hers then?'

'No,' he shook his head. 'I didn't see the sense of bothering her in her condition.'

'She wouldn't have minded and it would have been no troub-' Before she had the chance to finish her sentence, he had turned his back on her and was already making his way to the door.

He turned to look at her. 'See you later tonight, hopefully with some good news. Your mother has already signed the necessary documents for me.'

'When?' She couldn't believe this.

'Earlier this morning, I took them to her room.'

'But you said you didn't want to bother her and besides if you were ready to do that why couldn't you ask for use of her carriage?'

He smiled. 'I just want to get this sorted as soon as possible and I'd already arranged for the cab to return like I said.' He shot her a disarming smile. 'See you later!' he said cheerfully parting with a wave that left her fuming in her chair.

She was going to have to see her mother to find out exactly what she'd signed up for. *Archie where are you when I need you?*

Chapter Twenty-Five

1885

"Our Lucy"

'Yer'll have to tread carefully, mind, Archie,' Bessie said, wagging a finger at him. 'Don't want to be alienating our Lucy now, do we?' He'd noticed that she'd referred to Lucy as 'our Lucy' a couple of times during his visit. Wasn't that who she really was though? *Their Lucy.* Although it didn't seem much like it at the moment. It was as if since going to America and returning, there was someone else in her place, someone he barely recognised any more. No doubt that Sheldon, or who whoever he was, had turned her head. But could she really be that naïve not to realise the fellow was after her fortune? What other motive could he possibly have? He obviously wasn't who he claimed to be.

'Yes, I realise that, Bess,' Archie said in exasperation, reaching out and touching her hand across the table. 'I will be careful. Now how about you?' He asked sipping his tea.

She nodded. 'I'm all right, thanks fer askin' about me though.'

'What about the boys? Do you see much of them nowadays?'

'Harry's married now and living in Scotland. His wife is having their first child,' she said dreamily. She put down her cup of tea, placing it on its saucer. 'Pity though it's too far for me to see them often, though I was invited for Christmas but if I went, I'd never get me pie orders out on time, so maybe I'll go in the New Year instead when business is a bit slower.'

'And Jacob?'

'Jacob, I haven't seen fer a while. Only sees him if he wants something. He's working at some posh bespoke bakery in the West End.'

Archie's brow lifted with surprise. 'He's gone up in the world then?'

'Aye,' she nodded. 'All pastries with frills on at exorbitant prices!'

He'd never forget how he was bullied by the brute when he was just a young lad. Jacob had scared the hell out of him by threatening to put him in one of the big ovens at the bakery once. He didn't want to be reminded of that either. 'I'll tell you what,' he said brightly as he feared Bess was now a bit lonely in her old age. 'How about I ask Adella if you can join us for Christmas? I'm sure she'd agree.'

Bessie's eyes sparkled with excitement at the thought of it. 'Do you think she would agree? I haven't seen her since the day I waved Lucy off at the quayside.'

Archie felt a sudden pang of guilt at the thought he hadn't been there at the time, but it hadn't exactly been his fault, had it? 'Don't you worry. Leave the arrangements to me and I'll be in touch, Bess.' He rose from his chair and stooped to plant a kiss on top of the woman's head. It was lovely to be around such a warm-hearted woman once again. Bess was stoic and steadfast, which were both good qualities that he needed in his life right now.

***

Stunned that her husband had abandoned her yet again, Lucy took her mother's carriage to Chatterton Court. She breathed in deeply as she took in the sweeping snow-capped scene before her of the imposing house and surrounding trees, as the carriage clattered up the long-curved drive, which thankfully had been kept clear. Soon the snow might disappear altogether as quickly as it had arrived. Snow had arrived early this year and although beginning to melt, she knew it would make a reappearance at some point before Christmas.

Would Archie be pleased to see her once again? She just wasn't sure. Following their chat in the garden that time, once at the dinner table, he'd barely spoken to her preferring instead to spend the rest of the evening speaking with Lady Fanshaw who had seemed only too glad of his company. But how could she have chatted with him easily anyhow with Sheldon's eyes on her? He had seemed possessive enough then but now he barely laid his eyes on her, she felt like a piece of furniture, like the Queen Anne wardrobe in their bed chamber, or a walnut book case in the drawing room, so every day that no one really paid attention to them, they were just there— in the background.

Baxter answered the door to her. 'Is Archie around, Mr Baxter?' she asked hopefully.

Baxter looked her up and down as if she were the last person he expected to call at the house. Had Archie said something to him?

'I'm afraid he's in Whitechapel on business, ma'am.'

Whitechapel? Why had he gone there? There was only one person they both knew living in that area and that was Aunt Bessie.

Baxter coughed, intruding into her thoughts. 'You're quite welcome to wait here in the drawing room until Mr Pomfrey returns, if you like, ma'am?' He quirked a silver eyebrow in her direction.

She smiled. Somehow, she could never get used to the Pomfrey surname. To her, he would always be Archie Ledbetter running through Whitechapel in his threadbare clothes and his oversized flat cap.

'Er, no thank you, Mr Baxter. Please inform Mr Pomfrey that I called and shall return later.'

'Will do, ma'am.' He bowed, making her feel very honoured. She remembered Mr Baxter when she'd been lowlier than him as a simple kitchen maid at the coaching inn and Archie had been his friend, calling to the basement of the big house he worked at in the posh part of Whitechapel when he'd delivered Bessie's pies there. Baxter had befriended the lad which really helped while he'd been having a tough time of it with Jacob, who had been bullying him mercilessly.

Lucy thanked the man, then took her mother's carriage into Crownley with a view to seeing a local woman who wasn't a witch exactly, but was thought to be able to detect a pregnancy through her methods, though what those methods were, she wasn't quite sure. Adella, apparently, had chosen to go to her when she was pregnant herself at the tender age of fifteen. Although she thought the visit would be a bit pointless as the sickness had now abated and she felt ravenous in the mornings once again.

Arriving at the village, Lucy asked around for the woman known as *Dulcie Grimes*. Dulcie, by all accounts, was what was known as a wise old woman and people went to her with all sorts of ailments. She mixed various lotions and potions in bottles and jars for people to take away with them, tailoring each one to a particular person's ailments and as a result, no two potions were the same. Some folk swore by Dulcie's methods, even preferring hers to the local doctor's at times. The difference between her and any doctor was that she didn't charge for her services. People often left gifts on her doorstep, such as a freshly baked fruit cake or a bundle of sticks for her fire as a reward for her services, but more often than not, she was just happy to have been of assistance in their hour of need.

'Dulcie Grimes?' An elderly stooped lady who was stood with the aid of a wooden walking stick, replied to Lucy's request. 'Yes, she lives in the little cottage beside the river. You'll more than likely find her in as she hardly goes out these days.' The woman pointed her bony finger in the general direction.

'Thank you, very much,' Lucy said, delving into her drawstring bag to reward the woman with a silver sixpence for her trouble.

'Much obliged, ma'am,' the woman replied as she revealed an uneven set of teeth. Lucy felt a great deal of compassion for the woman as she went about her way, hunched up and taking slow, quivering steps with the aid of her roughly whittled walking stick.

The walk over to the riverside was quite pleasant, the snow had melted the past couple of days and the slush had all but dried up apart from pockets here and there. The sky was a cerulean blue and white clouds scudded overhead. The stone cottage with its thatched roof had a homely, yet mysterious appearance, as grey smoke billowed from the chimney. Dulcie was home as expected then.

Taking a deep breath, Lucy rapped on the woman's wooden front door.

'I'm coming! I'm coming!' she heard a croaky voice call out to her.

She stepped back as the door swung open to reveal the strangest little woman she'd ever seen in her life. She couldn't have been much more than four foot five inches in height, which made Lucy feel ginormous in her company. The woman's silver white hair hung long and loose on her shoulders. The dress she wore was every colour of the rainbow and appeared to have been stitched together out of old garment offcuts.

'Hello, dearie?' she said, her vibrant blue eyes shining brightly, belying her age and appearance. Those were wise, intelligent eyes, Lucy thought. 'What brings you to my door?'

'Hello. I was hoping you might invite me inside so I can tell you, Mrs Grimes,' Lucy said. She didn't want anyone to overhear them even though there was no one around, you just never knew.

'Come on in then, dear. I am just brewing up, would you like a cup?'

'Yes, please,' said Lucy fancying a nice cup of tea. What she was presented with instead was a thin hot drink which looked a little grey-green in colour with lots of bits floating in it as she took a seat at the woman's kitchen table.

Dulcie smiled. 'Don't worry, it won't do yer no harm. It's nettle tea, it's good for you. It'll keep yer skin and hair in good condition and it's good for you if you're with child? That is why you're here, isn't it? To find out if you're pregnant?'

Lucy nodded. 'Yes. How did you know?'

Dulcie tapped the side of her nose with her forefinger. 'Don't need to be a genius to guess these things. Truth be told though, most young woman of around your age are here either to see if they're pregnant or because they want to get rid of an unwanted pregnancy.'

'But how did you know that I wasn't the latter?'

'Because you ain't got that distressed look on your face that those sort have. Often, it's because they have too many mouths to feed back home and they want rid. I have to say though, I'm not into that sort of thing. I'll give them a cuppa and some advice and often that's all they need, but one poor soul...left here quite distressed she did, didn't know what to do next see and the pregnancy had interfered with that girl's mind.'

'What happened to her?'

'I'm sorry to say but the following day she was discovered floating in the river. She had decided to drown herself rather than face up to yet another pregnancy. Course I blamed myself as I hadn't helped her get rid of the baby and now there were two deaths instead of one, but the truth is I just make potions to help folk, I wouldn't know how to make a baby be born before it's time. I've delivered a few that were full term, mind you,' she said smiling.

Lucy took a sip of the tea which tasted earthy and warm and slightly peppery, not as bad as she'd first thought. She was beginning to warm to Dulcie and her herbal tea.

After chatting for a few minutes, the woman said, 'Now, because you've drank that tea you should be able to pass water?' She waited for Lucy's response.

'Y…yes, I suppose so.'

'Then you need to urinate in that pail there for me. She pointed to a white enamel bucket under the wooden sink.

Lucy did as told, feeling a little embarrassed but Dulcie left the kitchen on the pretence of stoking the fire in the living room to allow her some privacy.

When she returned and Lucy had tidied up her clothing, she peered into the bucket. 'My, my, you really needed to go, didn't you?'

Lucy smiled. 'Yes.'

'It's that nettle tea you see, it helps to flush out your system. Now what I'm going to do is mix it with something.'

Lucy watched as the woman went to a large cupboard in the corner and extracted a brown glass bottle with a cork stopper on top. She pulled out the cork and poured a few drops into the bucket and watched. 'If yer water changes colour you're pregnant, if not, then you have an empty womb,' she said confidently.

Lucy felt as though the wait took forever when in essence it was probably only a couple of minutes. The woman then looked up expectantly at her. 'Did you want a baby did you say?'

No, she hadn't said. 'I, er, I'm not too sure,' she said, which was the God's honest truth.

'Then you won't really mind that you're not pregnant, dearie. Maybe it will be a blessing for you and to remember to take a little care in the future.'

Lucy nodded slowly as she absorbed the woman's words. Not pregnant then. 'How accurate is that method though?'

The woman screwed up her features and for a moment, Lucy thought she'd upset her, but she'd just been thinking. 'It's a very successful test in my experience. Mostly this method turns out to be correct.'

'I see.'

'Only once or twice I've got it wrong. I ended up telling one woman she wasn't pregnant but then she gave birth to twins,' she chuckled. 'Another one I told her she was pregnant when she was not. It turned out though that woman had some sort of growth inside her which was something like a pregnancy. It turned out be a large mass containing hair and even a tooth! But whatever it was, it wasn't a baby, just a trick of nature...'

Lucy shuddered at the thought of it. 'I see.'

'I would suggest that if you have any more pregnancy symptoms in a few weeks that you return here as I can tell for sure by then by touching your tummy.'

Lucy nodded. 'Thank you, Mrs Grimes. I'll do that if there are any more. By the way, you predicted my mother was pregnant with me years ago.'

'Did I?' She looked thoughtful for a moment as if wondering who Lucy's mother was. She rubbed her chin in contemplation.

'Yes, Adella who married Nathaniel Knight.'

'Ah, of course!' she said, holding up an index finger in surprise. 'I do remember. That all turned out well in the end. I know Mr Knight wasn't your father but if ever a couple deserved one another, it was those two. I was so sad to hear of his sudden passing. He was a great benefactor to this village.'

Lucy smiled, so glad she had met the woman who had predicted her birth into this world.

***

Archie had found out some more interesting information following his trip into the city where he'd gone to visit one of his Uncle Walter's friends who was an esteemed doctor and high up on the medical board. Edward Hillings had told him that there was no question about it whatsoever, if it were discovered that Sheldon was an imposter and that he was manipulating various situations for his own ends, he would be struck off as a doctor. Archie had smiled to himself at the thought of that. Hillings had said he would write a letter to the medical board at The Eastvale Community Hospital in New York to inform them of the man's misdemeanours and the evidence gathered.

Archie, you're enjoying this a little too much, he said to himself. Another idea he'd had was that he should return to The Grouse and Peacock Inn to ask a favour of Bella and it wasn't of the sexual sort either.

He was still smirking to himself as his mind ran through giving Sheldon his comeuppance when his carriage drew up outside his house, to see one he recognised already parked there. Adella? What did she want with him? But he was pleasantly surprised to see it was Lucy who was waiting for him in the drawing room and not her mother.

'Oh Archie, I've been a fool,' she said, walking towards him as he instinctively took her into his arms.

He lifted her chin to look into her tear stained eyes. 'What makes you say that?'

She let out a shuddering breath. 'It's Sheldon, he's up to something and I think it involves Mama's money.'

Should he tell her that he had his own suspicions about that? 'Come and sit down near the fire and I'll ask the maid to fetch some tea and hot buttered crumpets for us, that will make you feel better. It always did when you were a young girl.'

She nodded at him gratefully. 'You always did know me so well, thank you.'

They chatted easily with one another for some time and it became clear they were on the same page but something Lucy did not know was that Sheldon wasn't who he said he was. The expression on her face changed as Archie explained he had some evidence to show her from a book he'd taken out from the library.

'The man is a fraud, Lucy. He's not who he claims to be.'

'B…but an imposter?' Lucy's voice trembled. 'But how can that be? I mean I know he mentioned something about having a different name to write his books. He explained all that to me. It's a pen name.'

'The one who wrote that book about the poor folk of Whitechapel is not the same man you are married to, I'm afraid.' He rose for a moment to go to the book case and selecting one, he passed it to her. 'I'm sorry to be the one to tell you this. Please look at the final page.'

She leafed through the final pages of the book until she found the one with the biography and the sketch of the real doctor: Sheldon

Harper Brown. Looking up at Archie as he stood near the fireplace, she asked, 'Then who the hell am I married to?'

'If you are really married to him at all then, Lucy.'

'Pardon?' Her hand went automatically to her chest as if she were in pain.

'Breathe, Lucy. Take some big deep breaths and let them out again.'

She did as told. 'I...I just don't understand this.'

'He might even have fake identification documents.'

'Oh, my goodness, I've just thought of something!'

'Yes?'

There was a woman who turned up at the tea room in Auburn in New York. She was all dressed in black as if in mourning. I went to the ladies' room and she appeared to be having some sort of heated conversation with Sheldon while I was gone. Then they both disappeared outside. There was something so odd about it all. They didn't notice me staring at them as I stood well back behind a wooden lattice screen.'

Archie frowned. 'That's strange.'

'Sheldon seemed to go very pale when that woman entered the tea room and without them seeing, I watched as she stood over him. He seemed very uncomfortable indeed.'

'A disgruntled patient, perhaps? Archie quirked a brow of derision.

'No, I don't think so. I have a feeling she was someone he knew very well indeed.'

'Did you bother to question him about her?'

She nodded slowly. 'Yes, eventually. He made out she was an ex-fiancée of his who had recently become widowed. But even so, I have my doubts he was telling me the truth.'

'What did his mother say about him while you were at the house?'

'Not an awful lot. Just things about his father dying when he was young and how he wanted to become a doctor after that. The strange thing was she didn't refer to his book or his previous journalistic experience. She made his writing sound as if it were more of a hobby rather than a vocation.'

Archie nodded thoughtfully. 'And do you believe he really is a doctor, too?'

'I believe so. His mother thinks he is and the physician my grandmother visited who is a friend of his, seemed to verify it was so. It's all so confusing. He must be a doctor though as the matron addressed him as Doctor Harrington that time I took Grandma to the hospital. That unnerved me as he'd told me his name was Sheldon Harper Brown but he had an answer for that of course.'

'Lucy whatever you do, you must stop your mother from handing over any money to that man,' Archie said forcefully. 'We don't know for sure who the hell he is!'

Lucy's face paled. 'She's already signed some sort of documentation this very morning.'

Archie sighed in frustration. 'But has Adella handed anything over as yet?'

'I questioned her about it when Sheldon left for the city, so I don't think so. She claimed she was only asked to sign the forms to allow the man access to some information at the bank.'

'Then maybe we are not too late after all,' Archie declared hopefully.

Chapter Twenty-Six

1885

"Please Don't Sign!"

'Mama!' Lucy called across the long passage way back at Meadowcroft Manor. Her voice echoed off the walls which gave the place a feeling of eeriness. 'Mama! Where are you?'

She heard the drawing room door creak open and instead of Adella standing there as she hoped for, it was the large looming figure of her husband. 'What's wrong, honey?' he asked as she walked with trepidation towards him. How could she possibly tell him she had come to warn her mother about not parting with any money? Her heart began to thud mercilessly and she hoped he wouldn't hear it as it pounded in her ears like a base drum.

'Where's my mother?' she asked breathlessly.

'She's in the drawing room, she was just about to sign another document for me so that the broker can sort out her finances...'

Lucy brushed past him almost knocking him out of the way, much to his surprise.

She entered the drawing room to find her mother sat at the escritoire with a fountain pen poised in her hand. 'Have you signed that yet?'

Adella looked up and smiled. 'I'm just about to.'

'Then please don't. At least not until you have a lawyer present.' She noticed now that Sheldon was at her side, his mouth agape in horror.

Her mother let out a little giggle as she wavered with the pen over the document. 'Is this some kind of joke, Lucy?'

'I'm afraid it's not,' Archie said as he followed Lucy into the room.

'Will someone please tell me what's going on here?' Adella's eyes widened.

'You'd better ask your *son in law*!' Archie spat out the offending words.

Adella frowned. 'Ask him what, precisely?'

'What plans he has for your money, Adella!' Archie shouted. He glared at Sheldon, who by now was walking head down towards the large arched window as if he couldn't believe what was going on, and was trying to compose his thoughts as to how he might turn this situation around.

Adella flung the fountain pen down on the writing desk as if it was suddenly too hot for her to handle.

She turned her head towards where Sheldon now stood facing them all in front the window. He slowly shook his head.

'You have to believe me, none of this is true. Archie is trying to discredit me as he's jealous that I married Lucy. It was me she really wanted and not him.' He shot Archie a look of disdain.

Sheldon's words couldn't have wounded him more deeply if they were well sharpened arrows from the swiftest of bows. But he had to think of Lucy and her mother's welfare right now and not himself. 'He's after your fortune for himself, Adella, and your daughter's inheritance.'

'No!' shouted Sheldon. 'I wanted you to invest the money wisely.' He turned to Adella. 'I don't need any money as I'm a celebrated author back home.'

'Rubbish!' Archie flung up his arms in mid-air. 'Author, indeed? You aren't the author of that book about the poor folk of Whitechapel, someone else is! I've seen the evidence for myself and so has Lucy.'

'B…but you can't have?' Sheldon was now looking at a loss for words. He ran a finger under the collar of his shirt as if it were choking the life out of him.

'Yes, I paid a visit to the library and managed to obtain a copy. Oh, it was very well written all right and by someone who should be celebrated for his great penmanship and research, only that person wasn't you! I've seen the sketch and biography at the back of the book and the author looks nothing like you. In fact, he's a great deal older with several children and a wife he's been married to for years!'

Put that in your pipe and smoke it! Thought Archie.

'I…I can explain,' said Sheldon.

But before he had a chance to say any more on the subject and try to dig himself out of a very deep hole indeed, Archie said, 'Oh you'll explain all right. Explain this then…'

Sheldon frowned.

'You can come in now!' Archie shouted.

Bella from The Grouse and Peacock swept in through the door in her finest day clothes which were garish to the eyes. Her bright red damask dress with low black frills, the stench of strong perfume clinging to her, and rouge applied to her cheeks, made it quite obvious who and what she was.

Sheldon stared at her and blinked hard.

Bella was Archie's trump card.

'Archie, who is this lady?' Adella demanded to know. 'And why have you brought her into my home?'

Archie smiled. 'All will be revealed and Lucy already knows about her.'

Lucy nodded. 'Yes, I do. You know Bella really well, don't you Sheldon? Or whatever your name is?'

Sheldon's cheeks flamed and he shook his head vigorously. 'I've never seen this dame before in my life!'

'That's not what you said to me last night when your hands were all over me, Sheldon. In fact, I think you referred to me as your *fanciful floozy*!' Bella put on a mocking tone of voice which amused Archie as she tossed back her mane of dark curls, her eyes flashing with anger at his denial. 'Insatiable he was, wanted to keep going all night long.' She smiled salaciously, hands on hips, obviously enjoying the trouble she was getting him in to.

'And how many times has Sheldon used your services, Bella?' Archie asked.

'Oh, loads of times. He's been using the girls' services for the past couple of years whenever he's been in the country. He's very well-known upstairs at The Grouse and Peacock, only he's referred to there as Mr Adams. I'm his favourite though as I can satisfy his every need and believe me, he does have some peculiar, how shall I say, foibles…' She tossed back her head and laughed in his face.

'Though Dora's the girl for all those perverted pleasures, isn't she, Sheldon?' Archie realised she was enjoying this as much as he was.

Adella's jaw slackened then she closed her mouth. 'I don't think there's much more to be said then regarding signing this document. I refuse to do it as I don't wish to have my affairs handled by someone who regularly cheats on my daughter at some sort of whore house!'

'Very wise an' all!' chipped in Bella.

Adella opened her desk drawer and taking out a sovereign, stood and whispered something in Archie's ear. He nodded at her and handed the coin to Bella. 'Thank you,' he said. 'You may leave now, the cab driver will take you back to the inn.'

Bella beamed. 'Thank you, it's been a pleasure doing business with you, Mr Pomfrey. And you, *Mr Adams!*' she scoffed as she left the room. Her chuckles could be heard echoing all the way down the hallway.

'Now who the hell are you really?' Lucy turned towards her husband, demanding to know the truth. The vehemence of her tone of voice took Archie by surprise.

It was no use. Sheldon, or whoever he really was, had little choice now he had been caught out fine style. His face paled. 'Do you mind if I sit?'

'Go ahead, please do,' said Adella in a softer tone than her daughter.

He sat in the upright chair near the window as the others stood looking down on him, eagerly waiting to hear the truth.

He huffed out a breath. 'My real name *is* Sheldon Harrington.'

'Are you really a doctor?' Lucy asked.

'Er, yes. I am a doctor but not as important as I've led you to believe. I'm quite a junior doctor really as I began my studies later in life. No one at the hospital knows me as Sheldon Harper Brown I'm known there as Doctor Sheldon Harrington.'

'So that's why that lady at the Eastvale Community Hospital called you by that name which confused me at the time?'

'Yes.'

'So why did you decide to impersonate the author Sheldon Harper Brown?' Archie wanted to know.

'Once, someone at the hospital asked me if I was him as they confused the name as we're both doctors called Sheldon and our surnames begin with the same letter. I'm afraid that when I went to England and people asked me about myself, I spoke about Sheldon the author more than Sheldon the junior doctor.'

'Just like you did with me on the steamer ship!' shouted Lucy, her chin jutting out in anger. 'But your mother seems to think you have risen up the ladder as a doctor. She gave me the impression you are an esteemed physician?'

Sheldon let out a long sigh. 'Yes, I'm afraid I have given her that impression as I didn't want to disappoint her. I failed my exams a couple of times so had to retake them over the years. Also, I wanted to impress you Lucy, that's why I deceived you. I wanted you to like me.'

'But I did like you and I'd have accepted you for who you were. I really gave my heart to you and you abused my affection by going behind my back with various ladies of the night.'

He shook his head. 'There are no excuses for it other than I found it difficult to be intimate with you as I felt you were too good for me.'

Archie flung himself at Sheldon, grabbing him by the collar of his jacket and hauling him onto his feet. 'That's no excuse to treat someone like Lucy that way. You've been living a lie and I've asked someone to find out if you and Lucy are really married. And another thing…you'll probably be struck off as someone my uncle knows has written to the medical board at your hospital.'

Sheldon, who was visibly shaken by now, lowered his head in shame. 'I deserve it all, I know that. I didn't deserve you, Lucy.' He said looking at her. 'And no, we're not legally married, we never could be.'

'B…but how so?' Lucy felt tears spring to her eyes. She'd had intimate relations with him a couple of times so now she was no longer a maiden. He had robbed her of her virginity.

'Because I am already married.' He put his head in his hands as if trying to hide his face.

'What!' Adella looked ready to pick up the large ornamental vase behind her and smash it over his head in anger.

'Wait!' shouted Lucy. 'I've just realised who you are married to. It's that woman who you spoke to at The Rosie Lee Tea Room, isn't it?'

He looked up at her and nodded slowly. 'Yes. The one I told you was my fiancée some years ago?'

'Yes, when I went to the ladies' room I saw you speaking animatedly with one another, she didn't look very pleased. Then you followed her outside as if to speak to her in private.'

Sheldon looked shocked. 'I never realised you'd been watching us so intently.'

'So, how long have you been married to her?' Archie demanded to know.

'About ten years, but I lied to Mother telling her we were actually divorced.'

Archie frowned. 'Is your wife in on this fraudulent thing you've been up to? A co-conspirator as it were?'

'Heavens no, she is innocent in all of this. I hate to admit it but I ran out on her a couple of years ago and she's been after me ever since for money to keep her. When I left her that day she chose to dress in black as she once told me she now feels like a widow, bereaved and abandoned to bring up the children alone.'

'Children?' Lucy blinked profusely. 'Oh, my goodness. What sort of man are you? To do this to me is one thing but to desert a wife and your young children is quite another!'

Seeing her like that, Sheldon stood and hovering near Lucy appeared to be just about to take her into his arms to comfort her, but Archie stood in his way to warn him off. 'I think it's time you packed your bags and left here. You've had enough hospitality from Adella and Lucy. Enough to last a life time, in fact!'

Reluctantly, Sheldon nodded. It was obvious he didn't want to leave but what other option did he have?

'Lucy,' said Archie, thinking maybe he'd overtaken the situation, 'do you need to speak with Sheldon in private before he leaves?'

Looking up at Archie with tears in her eyes and then across at the man she'd thought was her husband, she said, 'I've no more to say other than please don't dupe any more unsuspecting women, Sheldon. And is your mother really as ill as you claimed she was?' He said nothing, just shook his head. Angrily, Lucy shouted as she pointed her finger at him. 'You misled me to believe she was seriously ill and we'd need to marry in a hurry, how could you, Sheldon?' He turned away and headed towards the door as if all the life he had inside him had slowly ebbed away.

So, he'd used his own mother as a motive to rush her into marrying him. Unbelievable!

Sheldon left the room with his head lowered in shame, and a few minutes later, they saw him walk through the hall way with a couple of carpet bags of his belongings. 'Hey!' shouted Archie. 'We'd better check those bags before you leave in case you've taken the best silver.'

'Leave him be,' said Adella wisely. 'Let's just be glad that he's leaving Lucy's life for good and our inheritance is intact.'

Archie nodded as he heard the man shut the front door behind himself. 'Should have made him walk through the servants' entrance,' he said wryly.

At that moment, Lady Fanshaw descended the stairs after her nap. 'What have I missed?' she asked, rubbing her eyes.

Archie didn't know whether to laugh or cry. This had been an ordeal, particularly for Lucy to learn she wasn't married to Sheldon and he wasn't the man she thought he was either, but he was prepared to help her through it all, beside her all the way.

Chapter Twenty-Seven

1885

"Christmas Eve"

Preparations were in progress for Christmas festivities at Meadowcroft Manor. The hallway had been decorated with swathes of holly and ivy and a beautiful Christmas fir tree adorned with various shiny baubles and flickering candles, stood on display to welcome visitors to the house. Although it would be a quiet Christmas this year due to the death of Nathaniel Knight, Lucy was pleased that there would be a small gathering. Her heart no longer ached for Sheldon as waking up to the fact he was a fraud made her angry, not sad. In reality, he'd left the relationship after he'd married her because at the end of the day, it wasn't love he was after but her money. Still, he'd get his comeuppance by being struck off the medical register and might face a term of imprisonment for bigamy. Although he deserved all that was coming to him, she did feel sorry for his mother and for the woman he'd really married and then abandoned. No, she wouldn't miss Sheldon one little bit.

Though there was one person she missed dearly. She had gone to Whitechapel to find the woman after the news about Sheldon had come out. It was there she had longed to be, taking a cup of tea with her Aunt Bessie in her warm and cosy kitchen but when she'd arrived, there was no sign of life and she feared the worse.

'Archie,' she said as they sat around the table waiting to be served up a Christmas Eve feast of a honey glazed boiled ham and seasonal vegetables as Adella and Lady Fanshaw sat opposite them, 'I'm really concerned about Aunt Bessie. That man turned my head so much I couldn't see the wood for the trees and I failed to maintain contact with her after leaving for America and returning home here...'

Archie nodded and taking her hand in his said, 'Well, if there's anyone who will understand it's her. She might have gone to Scotland to visit Harry as his wife is expecting their first child.'

'Oh, I never knew that...' She felt a dull ache at not having kept abreast of things and a tear slowly trickled down her cheek. Throughout the meal, her appetite was limited and although Archie made attempts to lift her spirits with the odd quip here and there, the truth was she felt a little lost. By the time the pudding arrived she was hoping to make her excuses and head off for her bed by feigning a headache when she noticed the maid standing nearby.

'Please ma'am, your visitor is here,' Hetty said looking at Lucy.

'Visitor? But who can that be?' For a moment she wondered if Sheldon had the cheek to return on Christmas Eve and beg her forgiveness.

'Go and see who it is,' Archie urged.

Tentatively, she stood and made her way, walking behind Hetty into the hallway. There, standing well wrapped up in a blue woollen coat and large hat, was the person she'd longed most to see. Her shining eyes misting with tears as she gazed at Lucy. 'I figured I'd best call to see you after Archie came to see me the other day.' She held out her arms for Lucy to go into and they hugged one another for the longest time. Lucy felt like all was well at last. All the confusion and pain from the past few weeks simply melted away.

'Oh, Aunt Bessie, I'm so pleased to see you and I am sorry I never called to see you when I returned to England.' She sniffed loudly trying to hold back the tears that were threatening to spill.

'Aye, well Archie explained all that and he asked your mother if I could come fer Christmas dinner tomorrow, so she's kindly going to put me up overnight. Is yer hubby still 'ere? Archie told me there was some trouble.' Her eyes scanned the room as if in search of the man.

Lucy looked at Archie and smiled. Archie grinned back at her, knowingly. Of course, he was behind it all. He'd set up this meeting for her, she might have known.

'No, and apparently we were never even married in the first place. I'll explain all later but I'm so pleased you're joining us, Aunt Bessie. I did call to see you the other day and I was devastated that you weren't in.'

'I've been staying at Archie's house as a surprise for you. Archie told me all about yer husband.'

'Did he?' For a moment, Lucy wondered what had occurred. Archie's attention was caught by Lady Fanshaw who appeared to be asking him something.

Bessie took her chance to speak to Lucy in confidence. 'Aye. He called to see me as he was worried about you, now there's a man what really loves you and you should never let him go.'

Lucy's heart melted at the thought of what he'd done for her. 'I realise that now, I was blinded by my affection for Sheldon. I realise now that it wasn't love I had for him, real love is what I have for Archie. It's not about shining stars and fireworks, it's about feeling good to be in that person's company and realising they love you so much that they just want you to be happy, even if in doing so they sacrifice their own happiness in the process…' She swallowed a lump in her throat.

'Well now the blinkers are off, whatcha going to do about it, gal? Accept his proposal at long last?'

'I don't know if he'll ever ask me again,' Lucy said sadly. Behind stood Archie quietly, without her realising it.

'I've a feeling he might ask you again sooner than you think!' Bess winked over Lucy's shoulder at Archie who winked back at her.

Whatever happened in the future, Lucy was safe now with a family who adored her and a man who would give her the world wrapped up in a shiny red bow if he could.

In the distance, she heard the carol "God Rest Ye Merry Gentleman" being sung outside the door, giving her a warm Christmassy feeling deep inside as she thought of the times the carol singers called to her grandmother's home on Christmas Eve and they'd been invited into the kitchen afterwards for a glass of sherry and a mince pie each.

'I'll go and answer them now,' Hetty said excitedly, swiftly making her way to the door and opening it, framing the carol singers in the doorway with their lanterns and song sheets in their hands. Snowflakes had begun to settle on their clothing and it was perishing cold, but the singers didn't mind as they were used to being invited into steamy kitchens by folk as soon as they'd sang for them. Lucy thought it was as if they were singing just for them at Christmas as it was going to be the best one ever for her and Archie, she could feel it in her bones. It was then, Lucy felt Archie take her hand as he led her to the doorway to watch and listen as everyone else followed up behind them.

'Merry Christmas, Lucy,' he said tenderly, as he pulled her towards him, softly kissing her cheek. 'You know how much I love you, don't you?'

She looked up at him seeing the love light in his eyes which mirrored her own love for him, and she nodded and smiled. It was good to be home at last. 'Merry Christmas, my love,' she replied. Whatever the future held for her now, as long as Archie was by her side, it didn't much matter. They planned on taking their time to become familiar with one another once again, rekindling their romance, and who knew what 1886 might bring? Wedding bells she hoped.

Printed in Great Britain
by Amazon